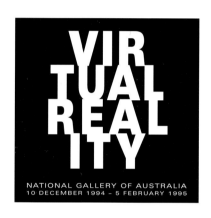

VIR
TUAL
REAL
ITY

NATIONAL GALLERY OF AUSTRALIA
10 DECEMBER 1994 – 5 FEBRUARY 1995

CONTENTS

CONTENTS

The title of the exhibition has been taken from new technology — not for the sake of that technology, but for the widespread promise of new ways of perceiving and interacting with the world.

What is 'real' experience in a world of 'virtual' experiences? The routine of daily life for most people is to wake to the beep of an alarm, jog or exercise to recorded music, eat processed cereal, take vitamin pills, drive to an air-conditioned workplace to work under artificial light, contact people by telephone, send messages by fax or e-mail, shop for cosmetics and this year's style of clothes, go to the movies, watch TV. People as they enact their lives already practise efficiently as artists: our world is constructed by human ingenuity. An ideal, romantic concept of 'reality' (meaning 'natural' truth) hardly fits our experience. In physical appearance, as in action, we are cultural creations.

At the same time, we still feel compelled to ask what is real. Writing about the art of Imants Tillers, Rex Butler has this to say about art and 'reality':

Art is always critical in this sense: it opens up a certain perspective onto things, it inhabits a different space from that of this world ... Art is a kind of fictitious *doubling* of the world, much stronger than any attempt to realise it, to speak of it in terms of a real, whether 'virtual' or otherwise.

There is a widespread recognition that 'nature' has been lost or superseded. Some behavioural themes of the 1990s seem strangely feral and hauntingly superstitious. This is a time of freak behaviours, weird symptoms, anarchy, cultism and metaphysics based on irrational signs and portents. It has been a time of worldwide political upheaval, a widespread searching for national (and personal) identity in the distant past, through blood lines and the earth itself. It is a time of assessing what is important by emotional response (the logic being that what one feels *is*). This is also a time of cynicism. The information age which offers such disparate expert advice, such a diversity of first hand reports, has made doubt and critical distance a general condition. The vicissitudes of politics and the economy likewise have blurred and fragmented the social system which no longer seems a 'system' at all.

The notion of individuality has been reviewed, Generation X cultivating an individuality much more fragile and fraught with uncertainty than Kafka ever imagined. In the 1990s, individuality is described communally as 'attitude' — a capacity to recreate oneself variously and habitually, using the recognisable signs, slogans and short-term references from the surface of Western culture. Attitude is a gut reality, tuned by bodily conviction and assessed by others according to how 'natural' it is; nonetheless there is a recognition that individuality is performed, not innate. The body itself has changed:

which is to say that at some recent time between the existentialists and us, the body lost its charge as involuntary truth and became, instead, the richest social signifier — culture tied to nature. Generation X lives with the knowledge that gut reactions may not define a true self. In a society that scans body language, plays the game of subliminal influence, explains human psychology by social imprinting, and engineers genetics, the traditional reference points of individuality — those of the body, the senses, and dreams — no longer have a capacity to indicate an individuality born of nature. In an overt (quite possibly disillusioned) recognition of the imprint of culture on the senses, 1990s attitude is to be found almost exclusively within the skin of advertisement, old and new fashions, film, popular music, television, computer games, fast food, tourist brochures, and in the causes and cults on the flip side of contemporary culture.

Ten years ago, the artist Richard Prince, who collected slogans, logos and images of popular culture, was one of the first to observe:

It's not just recorded conversation that sounds rehearsed or staged. You know, the way it can come off sounding truer than it really is, I mean, for some of us, even in day-to-day conversation we tend to sound like someone else talking, we're so self-conscious already, so overloaded with information, we play-act with voices produced from sources other than our own.[1]

In the early 1980s, Prince was able to worry about 'self-consciousness', an 'on purpose' attitude; in other words he exteriorised the 'wonderfully unnatural' prior availability of 'the information we transport'. Experiencing a split between what he was — which included how he acted as a 'receiver' — and the material he fished, he did what he did out of attraction, not necessity.

It's really that state of consciousness ... a receivership. You're there. You're there and it sets up a certain degree of belief in a reality, a pseudo-reality whose effect, in some cases, can be felt really deeply because you have this willingness, this *desire*, to believe in what is less true.[2]

One decade later, there is no simple polarity between what is true and untrue. The relation is not between commodities and receivership but a conscious and deliberate interiorisation of the 'contemporary'. This puts attitude — or personal style — in a curiously complicit relation to commerce. Advertising is powerful because it is geared to advocacy; its profession is to arouse desire. According to Benetton's Advertising Manager, Jerry Goodis:

Advertising doesn't always mirror how people are acting, but how they are dreaming ... In a sense what we are doing is wrapping up your emotions and selling them back to you.[3]

The cynicism, the despair or, to some observers, the fostering comfort, of finding one's true self in Hollywood! The generation for whom the terrain of self-description and social communication is the fast-moving world of CNN television, entertainment and consumption, also concedes that there

INTRODUCTION

lies the standard of normality. The comfort of togetherness is provided by this culture, rather than by the speculations of specialised knowledge, or tastes cultivated in isolation, or class, profession, politics, family, or nature. Other 1990s alternatives are the archaic values of caste and language group, and the measureless spiritual realm of religion.

The parallel between art and attitude is evident. What has been less evident is the extent to which art has presented the reverse of the advertiser's promise of fulfilling dreams. By contrast to a shopping mall, the art of our time looks bleak. The popular arts are figuring our dreams; artists instead have represented 'reality'.

On closer examination, Sylvie Fleury's luxurious art of shopping is a scene of spillage and loss. Chris Burden's over-sized uniforms are more expressive of coercion than the absent bodies they are too large to clothe. The inexorable gravitational slide of wet paint on Dale Frank's paintings distorts that artist's handiwork. Ashley Bickerton's solid black ocean wave may be an image of an oil slick but is also a yoke for dark human thought. Benetton's poster image of a seabird covered in oil is the standard imagery of a damaged ecology. This image, and others such as the billboard of a burning car and a poster of an albino child isolated among black Africans — all discreetly labelled 'United Colors of Benetton' — utilise the familiar visual imagery of the press in ways that seem downright shocking. Merely through recontextualising these images Benetton has shown up a morality that allows fair reportage on prime time television but is profoundly discomforted by frank voyeurism in commercial propaganda. Hans Haacke, who made his point by refusing to be represented in *Virtual Reality*, seeks to unmask another sort of hypocrisy. The façade he wants to rip down is that of politics. He says, 'let's not be fooled. Behind the spectacle politics continues … if a policy is built on a fiction its results are nevertheless felt in the world of reality'.[4] For Haacke, *reality is humanity.*

There are other artists who take a stand by reality. The objects of Antony Hamilton's installation possess a quality of certainty: the hard evidence of what the artist searched for near Eucla on the edge of the Nullarbor Plain, and found represented in an oil drum, a kangaroo shooter's car hood and other significant objects. The question 'myth or miss' hovers over the installation as it did over the search. In Berlin, Janet Burchill and Jennifer McCamley used photography to record a Turkish meeting place in Kreuzberg where the Berlin Wall once stood; since the creators of the meeting place were never present, their records taken by stealth over more than a year resemble the records of archaeology or forensic science. One definition of reality is truthful report. The names from the specialised language of the 'derro' that Robert MacPherson printed on grey blankets are, he says, serious records of what 'my milieu has taught me, as I've moved in and out of different strata of society; from base (or so-called base society) to so-called higher levels'.[5]

Reality and a haunting absence are the subjects of many of the works in *Virtual Reality*. Richard Jackson's small room, in which each wall and the ceiling is a large clockface, excludes everything but the point-by-point passage of time. Time is this room's unavoidable content, form and context. In paintings reminiscent of maps, but telling a complex truth more closely allied to metaphor, Gordon Bennett indicates 'points of identification' which are 'the sites of memories that flow through the conscious mind informing and constructing our identity, our sense of self

(a remembering of our experience, our history etc)'.[6] Damien Hirst's glass showcase containing an office table, chair and ashtray, makes absence positively present. The absent protagonist in this work is matched by absent protagonists in works by Bickerton, Hamilton, Burchill/McCamley, Burden, and Haacke whose (literally absent) work, a back-lit photograph, *The freedom fighters were here,* hovers around a pregnant absence. These works have 'reality' as their nostalgic target, the quest for which gives power and meaning to the representation.

Literal truth has a strange way of merging with the most powerful fiction. Ronald Jones's modernist bronze sculpture marries the 'truth' of scientific diagrams — in this case a construction of the *DNA fragment from human chromosome 13 carrying mutant Rb genes also known as malignant oncogenes which trigger rapid cancer tumorigenesis* — and the iconic truth of the famous sculptures of Brancusi and Arp. In much the same way, Jeff Koons pairs the historical value of classical marble sculpture with the social role model of Hollywood.

As well as art, the exhibition incorporates entertainments and merchandise. An interactive computer game is in operation; a top model automobile, clothes, perfume and chocolates are for sale. A journey through the galleries offers a number of choices. Because the context is an art museum, we are led to ask why commerce and art have been put together.

In combining art and commerce in a gallery space, my thinking was around the function of art. Art has always interpreted life. It has also represented power. Art once served Church and State by educating, informing, frightening, exciting, enthralling and alienating its audience with the express intent of enhancing the power of rulers. In tribal society, the best tattoos and cloths decorate the chiefs; for centuries in Europe there was a close connection between art, religious observance and state power; with the rise of capitalism art served the middle classes but still continued its double act of commenting on life. To consume and to comment are complementary activities. The title *Virtual Reality* is another name for art, in this exhibition presented in both of its aspects.

Virtual Reality is designed to be experienced in a number of ways, through shopping, eating and drinking, playing and responding to advertisement and art. Christopher Chapman and I, with the education staff of the National Gallery of Australia, hope that *Virtual Reality* will be encountered with enjoyment and accounted seriously — according to a reckoning that is individual rather than through prepared headings of 'art', 'education', 'social message' and 'entertainment'.

MARY EAGLE
NATIONAL GALLERY OF AUSTRALIA

references

1. Barbara Kruger and Richard Prince, 'All Tomorrow's Parties', BOMB, No. 3, Winter/Spring 1982/3, republished in Betsy Sussler (ed.), BOMB: Interviews, San Francisco: City Lights Books, 1992, pp.6–13. **2.** Ibid. **3.** Jerry Goodis, Advertising Manager, Benetton, quoted in Les Black and Vibeke Quaade, 'Dream Utopias, Nightmare Realities: Imaging Race and Culture within the World of Benetton Advertising', Third Text, No. 22, Spring 1993, p.65. **4.** Hans Haacke in Paul Taylor, 'Interview with Hans Haacke', Flash Art, No. 126, February/March 1986, p.39. **5.** Robert MacPherson, written statement, 1994. National Gallery of Australia Registry file. **6.** Gordon Bennett, letter to Christopher Chapman, 6 April 1994.

Virtual Reality presents art works alongside product displays by commercial companies — leaders in the fields of telecommunications, auto-engineering and computing: it signals not only themes in contemporary art, but the cultural pre-eminence of information technology and virtual reality.

The incorporation into a museum space of commerce and industry informs us not simply about the context of the production of contemporary art, but also indicates the cultural conditions that generate particular types of viewers or consumers. As art changes, so too do the consumers of art in their abilities and expectations. Today's gallery visitor lives in a world of fast cars and fast food, experiences the whole world on a television screen, and may now be accustomed to spending time in the virtual spaces where internet communications take place. Such a postmodern identity is increasingly alienated from the passive, contemplative experience of viewing art in a gallery. Indeed, the point is often made that the quintessential postmodern cultural pursuit is not art but shopping. I shop therefore I am.[1] In a postmodern society in which identity is no longer something fixed and unchangeable, but rather something chosen, created, bought, the market place is the major site of creative activity: the place where we make ourselves. And it is there that we learn to deal with the mass of visual images — advertisements, publicity material, television imagery — through which desires are forged.

Some of the artists in *Virtual Reality* play upon the allure of the iconic symbols produced and circulated within consumer culture. Sylvie Fleury's *Eternity* exploits the product label to connect with a constituency used to dealing with sales packaging. And Jeff Koons has made a career out of art that touches the heart of the consumer: his plexiglas-encased Hoovers were, he claims, designed precisely to 'give the viewer a sense of economic security'. Both artists engage with an art consumer who operates on a daily basis in a world of merchandising. But their tactics raise the question of whether art collapses into consumerism at a certain point. Is an artwork any different from a shop window display? What happens when art and commerce are seen in conjunction?

There is one obvious difference between the art museum and the shop: the museum does not deliver the goods. Unlike the auratic shop window display, a work by Koons or Fleury promises to dispense nothing. Their shop goods are effectively pulled out of circulation, disrupting — short circuiting — the flow of consumerism. Koons turns this situation to advantage, attempting to create 'a state in which actual possession is deferred so desire can be sustained indefinitely'.[3] In this way, the consumer's desire for the object is exploited, but not satisfied.

Are we to believe, then, that artists merely flirt with consumerism, tease the shoppers only to deprive them of their buying power, the power which is crucial to the identity of the consumer? This would be the case if art simply functioned to freeze-frame the act of shopping, to preserve 'the state of The New' and thereby sustain desire in perpetuity.[4] But to assume that art simply suspends time is to disregard the effects on the object, and on the viewing of that object, wrought by the museum itself. When consumer produce is placed in a museum it is reinvested into a new economy: an economy of art, which does not operate (overtly, at any rate) on principles of commerce. Within such economy, the consumer of art is offered something *other* than the product — and thereby something more than unrequited desire. (It would be a perverse act of self-denial to go to a gallery if this was really all that was on offer!) In other words, the institutional setting provides the object with a brand new set of associations, so that we do not expect the same pay-off from an artwork as from a consumer product.

Art can, in fact, exploit the museum economy to alter perceptions of everyday objects. So long as an object is submerged in the everyday, its meaning is taken for granted and our perception of it dimmed. When it is removed to an unfamiliar context, we see it anew. Severed from its prior context, the object acquires a *strangeness*, an uncanny aspect, which functions to sharpen our perception of it.[5] The *estrangement* that results from dislocation, it has been argued, increases the 'difficulty and length of perception' so that one's response to the object as art exceeds or differs from one's response to the object in its everyday context.[6] In other words, a response to the art object must be more/other than the desire one has for shop goods.

Thus, when we see an L.A.P.D. uniform, taken off the streets (or removed from its even more familiar context of a television cop show or news item), it becomes an emblem of the Los Angeles riots, a fetish of power, and hence a means of questioning the way that authority is invested in the sign. When we see a desk, an ashtray and a packet of cigarettes encased in glass, the mundane trappings of the office are 'made strange' in a way that causes us to rethink our everyday encounter with work spaces. And when we see pristine vacuum cleaners in a plexiglas case, we do not experience them as a shop window display; the viewing process is extended and modified in a way that leads us to reconsider our response. We cannot perceive the objects as if they were in their everyday context because the ground is cut away from under them.

This is the effect not just of art, but of the institution; of the way the museum inflects its objects. Artists can utilise the museum space to create an apparently neutralising effect, but the museum is not in fact a neutral space: it is an institutional space which traditionally defines itself apart from the commercial world. It is able to make the commercial product appear strange precisely because it frames objects as precious rather than consumable.

But if the art museum makes us rethink objects through enacting a series of displacements, what happens when some of its found objects are returned to the market place? Here we have a shop in the middle of a museum, selling products which, in some instances, relate to the art on display: Eternity perfume, Benetton clothes, Kodak disposable cameras and video games. Rather than simply removing products from circulation and reinvesting them as high cultural icons, the art institution is now actively reinserting products into a commercial economy. In refusing the radical separation of museum culture from consumer culture, *Virtual Reality* acknowledges that the museum can no longer assert claims to separatism, or to cultural pre-eminence.

Art can question the 'reality' outside the museum, but since it does this by making its objects look weird, by depriving them of contextual significance, the museum can never claim to be offering a greater 'truth'. The museum, like all other cultural spaces, is only ever virtual in this sense: virtual because it does not uncover 'reality', it merely provides a space for yet another restaging of objects we all see and use on a daily basis.

In this respect, the museum vies with the other spaces of late capitalist culture, all of which function to stage their objects in new and innovative ways. The television commercial, the shop window display, the gallery installation, all work to produce meaning around their object. In its own terms, the story of shopping is no more bizarre than the story of art. It is only when the context is undermined, when chains of association are severed, that we become aware of what we habitually accept as the norm. Now, if art can show how strange the 'real' world is by relocationg objects, the process of 'making strange' can be reversed. Once the shop enters the museum, and sets up conflicting associations for objects, we may also come to realise just how strange is the practice of art making in the late twentieth century.

JILL BENNETT

references

1. *This reformulation of Descartes's epithet 'I think therefore I am' appeared in a work by the American artist Barbara Kruger.* **2.** *Jeff Koons,* The Jeff Koons Handbook, *London: Thames and Hudson, Anthony d'Offay Gallery, 1992, p.50.* **3.** *David Joselit, 'Modern Leisure' in Yve-Alain Bois et al (eds)* Endgame: Reference and Simulation in Recent Painting and Sculpture, *Boston, Mass.: ICA, 1986, p.83.* **4.** *Ibid.* **5.** *This process of altering perception of the familiar through 'making it strange' was elucidated by Shklovsky and the Russion Formulists, who employed the central concept of ostranenie, or defamiliarisation, to describe the function of art. See Tony Bennett,* Formalism and Marxism, *London: Methuen and Co., 1979.* **6.** *Ibid., p. 31.*

I believe artists must exploit themselves, and they must also take the responsibility to exploit the viewers.[1]

I believe the way to enter the eternal is through the biological.[2]

♡ *Jeff Koons has put Marcel Duchamp in the missionary position. With* **Made in Heaven** *he gave the term 'endgame' a whole new slant. For years working his way through a repertoire of approaches — the legacy of Marcel Duchamp's readymades and the paintings and sculptures of Andy Warhol — Koons has come to the realisation that to make art relevant he must take it into the realm where the desires and the doctrines of contemporary society are declared. Koons has discovered that in order to compete on this level he must present art with the same motivation as admen, rock stars and media hucksters. The enigma of the castaways of consumer society selected by Duchamp has been rejected for the more glamorous consumer products (or a simulacrum thereof) of Middle America. Duchamp's pieces spoke of mystery and in some cases of dematerialisation through reference to the fourth dimension. Koons's pieces smack of the world of Hummel and Lladro figurines and airport art which gleefully declare their superficiality and their seductiveness. Bogus metaphysics has ceded to cheerful marketing.* ♡ As Koons has said: 'Salesmen are today's great communicators. They are out there pushing cars, real estate, advertising. That is where the real morality is played out in society today.'[3] *His oeuvre consists of new products: vacuum cleaners encased in perspex vitrines and sanitarily lit by fluorescent tubes; basketballs suspended in 'humidi-cribs' of different densities of water; stolen images from Nike sportswear ads and alcohol ads which indicate levels of life-style; stainless steel castings of novelty whisky containers and inflatable toys, bar accessories and kitsch sculptures; larger-than-actual size porcelain and polychromed wood sculptures of everything from toys to a white Michael Jackson and his chimpanzee 'Bubbles'; and, more recently, the objects and paintings of his great piece of self-exploitation,* **Made in Heaven.** ♡ **Made in Heaven** *covers a number of works which include large canvases with silkscreened photographs of Koons and his wife Ilona Staller in the act of making love. Most of these carry titles which are in reality deadpan descriptions of the action: 'Jeff Eating Ilona (Kama Sutra)', 'Ice — Jeff on Top Pulling Out', 'Fingers Between Legs'. Interestingly, the paintings resemble film stills and in fact a film was to be made which would relate to the stills. The* **Made in Heaven** *billboard has all the hallmarks of a movie announcement, with the Koonses posed in a more demure position than the promise of the stills. However, the film scheduled for release in early 1991 never came to fruition. As a result the paintings of Jeff and Ilona remain as frozen moments of a film never made, much like the car crash and race riot paintings of Andy Warhol or the set-up photographs of Cindy Sherman.* ♡ *The series also includes a large polychromed wood sculpture of Jeff and Ilona in passion on a rock surrounded by a massive snake, playing out the roles of Adam and Eve.* **Made in Heaven** *premiered in the Aperto section of the Venice Biennale of 1990. When shown at Sonnabend Gallery in New York in late 1991, it included 3-D glass sculptures of Jeff and Ilona in similar positions in tinted glass as well as polychromed wood sculptures of puppies, poodles and Yorkshire terriers which give a bizarre innocence to the sexual acts that abound in the other pieces. The acts could be considered offensive and the effect pornographic, but they are portrayed in innocence — an innocence emphasised by the fact that Ilona is hairless, pure in clean white Fredricks of Hollywood lingerie, crowned with flowers and shoed with glinting metallic high heels.* ♡ *Jeff and Ilona are also manifest in marble.* Bourgeois bust *features Mr and Mrs Koons staring adoringly at each others' eyes while embracing, with Jeff's left hand caressing Ilona just below her right breast. He is naked and she is clothed only in strings of beads. They are the stars of their own show. Ilona — aka La Cicciolina (the pinchable one) — born and raised in Hungary, a pornographic film star and later member of the Italian parliament, is no stranger to the media; and Jeff Koons has underlined his artistic existence by flirting with and exploiting marketing hype. This is a marriage made on Madison Avenue, a McLuhan massage of the most literal order: 'Ilona and I were born for each other. She's a media woman. I'm a media man. We are the contemporary Adam and Eve.'[4]* ♡ *So where are we? — we the viewers, or should I say voyeurs, for that is all we are allowed to be. Koons's objects, like his enshrined sex acts invite us to partake visually but do not allow involvement. We are in the art gallery version of Home Shopping — we can look at the objects, we can be excited by their cuteness, their explicitness, but we can only buy them and place these objects around us. With* **Made in Heaven** *we are on the sidelines of sex as transcendency and, in Koons's case, we are witness to the ego in ascendency — the only true spiritual outlet in the world of hyper-marketing.* ♡ *There is something club-footedly romantic about* **Made in Heaven**, *with the purposely proplike settings, plastic flowers and butterflies, and totally artificial painted backdrops. The same is true of the subject matter of the puppies, the* **Popples,** *the* **Winter Bears,** *the flowers and even the stainless steel bunny. Underlying the inspiration of many of these works there is a twinge of nostalgia, a yearning for what is cute, what is artificial, what is safe. There is even a sweet sadness in the sex acts. La Cicciolina's slack-mouthed expressions of ecstasy also look like the expression of entrance into death. Jeff and Ilona could be construed as enacting the sexual dance of life, like some enactment of Ignatius Loyola's* **Spiritual Exercises** *or an exercise from Thomas à Kempis's* **Imitation of Christ.** *We, the observers, are like the sculpted members of the Cornaro family as they witness the ecstasy of St Teresa, Bernini's great theatrical enterprise in the church of S. Maria della Vittoria.* ♡ *If there is any truly transcendent matter here it is the line between sex, innocence and death. But such thoughts are easily cast aside when these scenes are included with the cute puppies and other sculptures. They are lovable. And yet! There is something grotesque about them: like many of Koons's other objects, they are magnified, they are oversized and they are surreal.* ♡ *There is something all of Koons's works share, from the vacuum cleaners encased in perspex and the basketballs floating in tanks with two densities of water to the puppies and stacked animals; but especially in the case of Koons's stainless steel casts. They are all remarkably clean. The utter cleanness of Koons's choices of surface are a wonder, whether it's a plastic, painted blowup bunny rendered in mute stainless steel or Cicciolina in virginal white with an exquisitely shaved pubic region. Koons himself declares his recognition of this with two of the* **Made in Heaven** *pieces. Both entitled 'Dirty', they show Jeff and Ilona in similar positions to those in the other* **Made in Heaven** *images, but here the participants are smeared with cosmetic dirt. The irony of fake filth is not just a visual pun, it is a tribute to the very element that is missing.* ♡ *Koons's works are products that conjure up a world 'in control' — an ideal world where everything is right. Post-porn-modernist, Annie Sprinkle hit a chord on seeing* **Made in Heaven** *in New York in 1991.* **'Alas, it is this search for sanitized perfection that is the one unsettling aspect of Koons's deceptively benign art. Call me paranoid, but the parallels between fascism's exaltation of the clean white neoclassical form and Koons are almost too uncanny.'**[5] *Not only that: 'Koons's love affair with everyday treacly romantic schlock is strikingly similar to the nostalgic hankering for the simple pleasures of true Bavarian folk art.'[6] The same values were exalted by the Nazis of the Third Reich. This is the underbelly of the works: a hint of the mildly addictive effect of the seduction of the cute and the desirable as tools of some Brave New World. It is this that brings Koons as an artist into the concerns of the twenty-first century.*

alan r. dodge

references

1. *Jeff Koons,* The Jeff Koons Handbook, *London: Thames and Hudson, Anthony d'Offay Gallery, 1992, p.34.* **2.** *Ibid., p.35.* **3.** *Ibid., p.32.* **4.** *Ibid., p.140.* **5.** *Annie Sprinkle, 'Hard-Core Heaven',* Arts Magazine, *Vol. 66, No. 7, March 1992, p.48.* **6.** *Ibid.*

Due to copyright restrictions we are unable to reproduce Made in Heaven *1989. This blank billboard is of the same dimensions. The original transparency has been supplied by Anthony d'Offay Gallery, London.*

JEFF KOONS

PRETEXTS: ACCENTS OF THE MODERN IN THE WORK OF SUSAN NORRIE

susan norrie *Elegance of taste.*
1991 oil on canvas 7 panels, each
152.0 x 61.0 cm. Private Collection,
Photograph Tim Marshall

susan norrie *Model seven
(from Room for error)* 1993 (detail)
oil on canvas 7 panels, each 152.0
x 61.0 cm. Collection the artist,
Photograph Tim Marshall ▶

◀ **susan norrie** *Elegance of taste.*
1991 (detail)

It is an integral precept of contemporary cultural analysis that human experience is conditioned by a world fibre-optically connected, an image world where information is instantaneously consumed, exchanged and revalued. Within this contested state 'consumption is increasingly synonymous with communication', 'interactivity' with 'shopping'.[1] It is argued that as a result of this condition the image has been confirmed in, and thereby enforces, a privileged position as the primary site of meaning and value. This description of the post-modern condition proposes that it is our destiny to live and become one with a preconstituted if ever changing reality where the temporal is flattened out and knowledge and feelings are severed from objective experience.

Read against this construction of post-modernity, the work of Susan Norrie presents itself as a dichotomy. It simultaneously confirms and resists the logic of this discourse. For in many ways she displays tendencies perceived as symptomatic of the post-modern. Her apparent preoccupation with surface and style for example; her free-ranging high and low culture borrowings from diverse moments in history; her recourse to photo-reproductive technologies or her concern

to highlight the image as a text — a play of signifiers culturally determined. And yet in isolation these characteristics of her work can be argued as being strategic interventions within the image and information marketplace, along with her foregrounding of the status of painting as commodity or her ironic reprioritisation of the object within and against the field of painting.

This marketplace, however, is adept at repositioning resistant images within the parameters of its inherent logic, thereby homogenising difference. Thus the unruliness of alternative representations is neutralised through their ultimate availability for consumption. Norrie's strategies, though, both co-operate and are reflexive and are consequently not easily visually contained. They function as an index: her vocabulary of images, forms and motifs continuously resurface within diverse temporal and spatial contexts.

Take for example the work *Elegance of taste* 1991 first shown in the exhibition *vis à vis* at the Nancy Hoffman Gallery, New York. Within that installation the work functioned as one of a number of conceptually linked but formally distinct units that included items of furniture, three–dimensional models, as well as figurative and non-figurative paintings. The work itself, in its periodic placement

of seven uniform panels, each presenting a different hue, is emblematic of a scale; a metaphor for harmony perhaps, as well as a recollection of the evocative fields of modernist abstraction. Emerging from the surface of each panel's simulated fabric covering is a maxim concerning the elegance of taste, set in cursive script.

This reference to a model of refinement and manners serves as an echo of an eighteenth-century sensibility. It is an echo that returns, if in a somewhat sublimated form, in the similarly seven-panelled work, *Model seven* 1993, first shown as part of the installation *Room for error* 1993 at the City Gallery, Wellington. The panels of this work also simulate surface conceits, their cool and antiseptic veneers visually abstracting the texts they shroud — historical recipes for embalmment.

Such repetition and interplay of form, surface, image and text has come to characterise Norrie's work. The transpositions involved here — between verbal and visual signifiers, between object, text and image, between panels, between distinct works

— exceed the spatial or the temporal. They suggest a locus for her work beyond representation. In this sense her works are incomplete, their contents fluid. Her forms defy closure and thereby function as visual residues deflecting attention onto the complexities of human response.

By tracing the trajectories of the modern, Norrie revises the relationship of the body to constructions of visuality. She plots a philosophical shift from the notion of the classical body, a body that is perceived in terms of its essential unity with nature and reason, to that of the post-modern body, the body without origin, externalised and maintained within a global field of images. Norrie interprets this shift with reference to critical moments. She emphasises the Enlightenment theories of the eighteenth century which distinguished sight amongst the senses — theories informed by the new spaces of vision opened up through advances in science and medicine as well as through the imaging of 'exotic' cultures. Further she relates these developments to twentieth-century modernism and implicates them in the modernist failure to break with history and achieve its utopian vision.

What is involved here is an exegesis of western models of vision and visuality that inform contemporary perceptions of

the body. In many of her works, such as *Elegance of taste*, these models of seeing are connoted through overlapping veils, thus suggesting an interdependence. But while Norrie interprets the philosophical histories through which sight has become privileged amongst the senses, her evocation of the body remains invisible and therefore she is able to by-pass the very models of perception she references. For the body is largely unrepresented in her work, seemingly absent. However a sense of its presence is hauntingly sustained; insinuated by its deferral to its surface and coverings, and significantly to its interiority — its fluids, its breath.

If the modernist movement sought to encompass the world within one history, post-modern discourse normalises that imperative by including all possibilities of difference within its multiple frames of reference. How then can we hear the accents of the modern that inform this discourse? This is the question Norrie asks. Like the process of embalming, her works speak of the surface and the visual collapse of time into one moment. But her concern is for what lies below the surface, what has been drained out. The allusion is to a transaction of knowledge that defies visual identification, that remains camouflaged.

Read as a collective set of operations, Norrie's interventions display strategic competence and begin to make problematic readily digestible theories of reception. But it is through her ability to divaricate and implicate the viewer in instances of cultural, sexual and personal difference, overlooked or not registered within the western historical narrative, that her work resists easy identification and thereby consumption.

Norrie accesses post-modern discourse to inform her practice as an Australian woman artist working at the 'recovered periphery' of the new world. But rather than invoke this model as an absolute description of the contemporary, she interprets its currency as an effect of the modern, thereby interrogating the pretexts of its shifting yet universalising claims to truth. It is ultimately through her enactment of a body that escapes representation that Norrie's work can be felt to resist the synthesised pulse of post-modernity.

gregory burke

reference

1. Jonathan Crary, 'Critical Reflections', Artforum, *Vol. 32, No. 6, February 1994, p.59.*

In 1989 the New Zealand sculptor Neil Dawson invisibly suspended a 4.5m diameter translucent globe high above the plaza of the Centre Georges Pompidou in Paris. *Globe 1989* was his component in the French world survey exhibition 'Magiciens de la terre'.[1] Modelled from the famous NASA photographs of the earth from space, *Globe* is made with the carbon fibre and polyurethane laminating techniques of New Zealand yacht builders. With the oceans left as spaces to allow light to pour through, and held together by its clouds, *Globe* displayed a simplicity and ease of appearance that made it hover, pure and inviolate, like a new parallel earth materialised in the sky. ● In Paris, Dawson managed to slip *Globe* like a cuckoo's egg (perhaps the New Zealand native Shining Cuckoo who sings 'Tuia tui tahia: Bind us together, let us be one'[2]) into the heart of French contemporary culture (and imagined hegemony). Yet all the while he denied the Centre Georges Pompidou the ownership implied by containment within the gallery. Instead, as it was the only work in the exhibition to be shown outside, *Globe* was owned by the 'International carnivale'[3] in the plaza. To this cosmopolitan, partially non-art audience, only New Zealand and Australia were visible; Paris was reduced to a provincial centre somewhere on the other side of the (art) world. Art did not need to be pre-known or paid for, cultural attitude was the thing and looking would suffice. ● In *Virtual Reality*, *Globe* is re-installed for the first time, held in a web of fine steel cables between the National Gallery of Australia and the High Court of Australia — poised between the symbolic heart of the art establishment and the third arm of government. Not just gallery visitors, but judges, politicians, tourists and workers alike are confronted by an illusionary world, that hovers between a simple sculptural object and a global view. A planet, isolated and delicate (the size of a big harvest moon), inhabits one of the most important structural spaces created by Australia Inc. 'If art contributes to, among other things, the way we view the world ... then it does matter whose image of the world it promotes and whose interests it serves.'[4] ● Without a mount and free of weight or scale, *Globe 1989* deliberately draws away from its imperial and scientific predecessors. (Both Australians and New Zealanders are well aware of being the farthest bits of pink.) This globe is literally transcendent, not only does it appear to triumph over the laws of gravity, but you must lift your eyes to see it, in much the same way as you look up at a Gothic rose window or the dome of a Renaissance cathedral. This is an island dweller's perspective: technically self-reliant and unafraid to see the world as an object *apart* from ourselves, like a quote from god — it is us up there. ● Like the 'real thing' (even better than), *Globe* is impossible to physically reach, it cannot be verified even as a work of art. In searching for its meaning we are bound to enjoy the unknowing and to ritualise it; to own the illusion at least, by taking photographs. Mr Kodak neatly completes the circle from image to object to image, from generic ownership (through constant reproduction) to ambiguous physical illusion and back, to a weird popular mimicry, a sort of mass pictorial deconstruction. The looking for meaning has become more important than the object itself (unless endless photographic documentation of our lives has become a substitute for the need to understand). ● *Globe* has the received qualities of a billboard in space. The image of the floating earth is repeated *ad nauseam* around the world to 'bring the world back home', so much so that no one product can claim it as its own. At least commercially and, I suspect, purely visually it has become a generic image. Free of specific meaning it is not a symbol, recognisable because it *tells* us something, rather *Globe* is a transformer ('read translation, rotation and reflection'[5]) larger in our mind's eye than in reality — a planet, (not) a mass media induced shared vision of creative and commercial involvement. ● So what people expect to see is the image anchored to a cause or product, always framed/contained and usually entitled. (In 1989 for the cover of *TIME* magazine USA, Christo wrapped a 40.5cm globe in polyethylene and rag rope to provide the illustration for the headline 'Planet of the year: Endangered Earth'.) What they actually get is an object — untitled and disengaged, recognisable because we (now instinctively) know what it is supposed to be, but also unbelievable as it asks us to believe an external 'visionary' view of the world that is also objective, an image that none of us (except for a few astronauts) has ever experienced. ● Sculpturally *Globe* seems to collect the space and light surrounding it to become a focus, a point where all the conceptual, sculptural, communal and political components of such a public work of art (and loaded architectural space) converge. It inhabits space much like an effigy, a sort of aesthetic sounding board, where artistic (and political) vision is not instructive or inclusive but allows you the space to reflect on what it means to you. It is what the artist likes to call the 'art of the possible' — it can be anything from a 'reminder of our fragile world in peril to a logo for Corporation Earth'.[6]

tim fisher

NEIL DAWSON

references

1. Magiciens de la terre, *Musée national d'art moderne — Centre Georges Pompidou, 18 May – 14 August 1989.* **2.** 'Te Tangi o te Pipiwhararua: traditional chant passed by Tangira Hotere to his son Ralph Hotere who in turn passed it to Colin McCahon who painted it into "The Shining Cuckoo" 1974.' Wyston Curnow, 'Colin McCahon: Borders, Barriers and Frames' (unpublished). **3.** Author's conversation with the artist June 1994. **4.** Hans Haacke in Sandy Nairne, State of the art: Ideas and images in the 1980s, London: Chatto & Windus in collaboration with Channel Four, 1987, p.132. **5.** James Ogilvy, Many Dimensional Man, *New York: Oxford, 1977, pp.46–47.* Quoted by Gregory Ulmer, 'OP WRITING: Derrida's Solicitation of Theoria' in Mark Krupnick (ed.), Displace/ment: Derrida and After, *Bloomington: Indiana University Press, 1983, p.53.* **6.** Jim and Mary Barr, 'Going Public'; Neil Dawson — Site Works 1981–1989, *Wellington: National Art Gallery of New Zealand, 1989, p.70.*

gordon bennett *Panorama (with floating point of identification).* 1993 synthetic polymer paint on canvas 137.0 x 167.0 cm. National Gallery of Australia. Purchased 1994

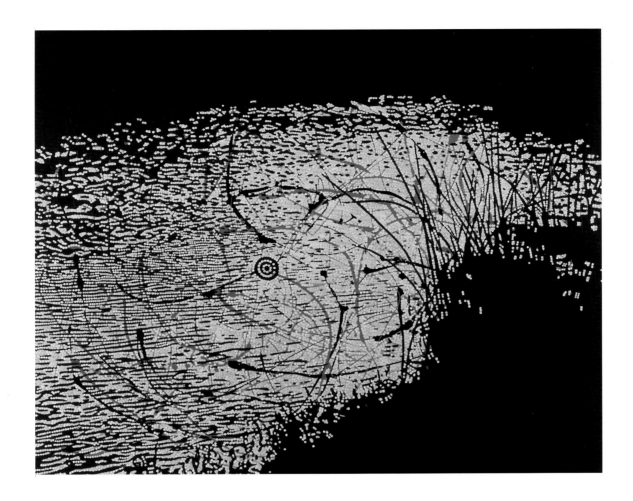

GORDON

In the long term, physics may well be seen as the greatest artwork of the twentieth century. In a field dotted with brilliant and paradoxical concepts perhaps none is so stunning as that of the Black Hole which sucks into its maw all matter and all light. Whether there is a sphere beyond a Black Hole is speculation — perhaps a mirror image of the universe is reconstituted on the other side. On the terrestrial plane, black is usually regarded as opposite to white, which is designated as signifying purity. For Gordon Bennett, an artist of Aboriginal and European background, such conceptual duality is a form of violence which splits the psyche of all. He notes that in western culture: **Black is the colour of fear, of emptiness ... As it is the colour of the void it must be filled; filled with the ideals of the west. Progress is a road through the void to utopia which waits over the horizon. Perspective is the compositional device that constructs a harmonious picture of progress. It pushes all that stands in the way to the sides in its headlong rush to the vanishing point.** [1] For Bennett, such matters are political imperatives generating the work he has done since 1986 when he quit his job in Telecom to study painting. His own psyche was inscribed with white culture. The revelation of his Aboriginality at the age of eleven began a process of the excavation of that part of his heritage which had been as mute as a Black Hole. ■ In *204 years*, Bennett overlays an icon of modernist reductive abstraction, Malevich's *Black square* (1915), with the whipped paint skeins of Jackson Pollock whose art tapped into the wellsprings of the psyche. The conjunction suggests a fertilisation of the void. In the context of Australian history, these marks also represent the scarification of the Aboriginal, both in their own rituals and as a result of torture by the White man. The datelines on the painting signify the European invasion of Australia and the recent Mabo land rights legislation (which acknowledges that Australia was not unoccupied in 1788, was not a *terra nullius*). Like bars of the *I Ching*, they also enigmatically present an = sign — an equality perhaps? The resolution of this potential new 'equation' is yet to be seen.

gordon bennett *Panorama: Crevice (with two floating points of identification).* 1993 synthetic polymer paint on canvas 137.0 x 167.0 cm National Gallery of Australia. Purchased 1994

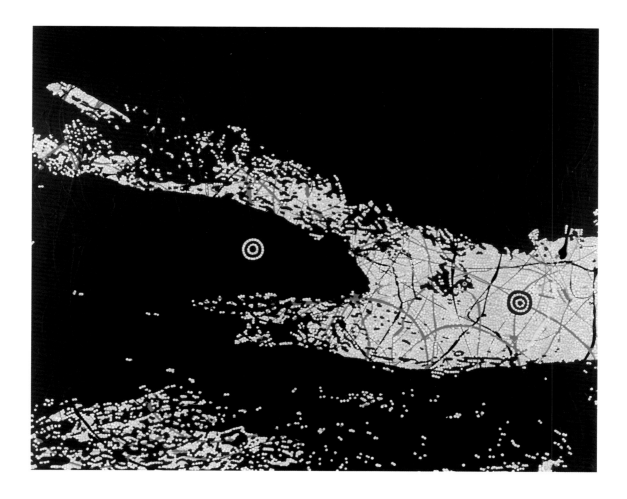

BENNETT

The *Panorama* paintings propose a new vision of the landscape. In western art a panorama presents a broad scenic view parallel with the horizon, and most typically centres on a one-point perspective in which the spectator is the apex — thus the consumer of the reality being presented. Bennett's panoramas are not consecutive; the two images hang one above the other. The traditional central vanishing point is as elusive as an electron in a cloud-chamber. A field of of scintillating dots and concentric circle motifs from western desert painting proliferate and consume the void. In the lower image *with two floating points of identification* the motif of whipped skeins of paint becomes the lightness of reeds on a riverbank. This is not a simple reversal but a perspective liberated from its fixed position. In the shifts from foreground to background, Bennett transforms the linearity of history (both art and colonial) into the cyclic dynamism found in Aboriginal art — also offered by that great 'other' for western culture, the spiritual metaphors of the east. As he says: **The points of identification are the sites of memories that flow through the conscious mind informing and constructing our identity, our sense of self, (a remembering of our experience, our history etc.). If one's mind can be seen as a landscape, then memories are like the rivers and streams that nurture it, that connect sites of significance to our sense of ourselves. All rivers run into the vast inland sea eventually, to evaporate and float away as clouds, to rain down again in another time and place, to once again flow and connect. This is the great cyclic 'panorama' of life, memory, experience.**[2] Bennett collapses the window box perspective and the unities of time and space so beloved of traditional western art — not to be sucked into a Black Hole but let loose on the free range of the mental ethernet. Ian McLean has seen this process as generic to postmodernism, using as his model that of the rhizome, a circuit which by ever dividing and proliferating 'explode[s] the prison house of difference and representation'. Everything from the macro to the microcosm 'can be articulated in the digitalised codes of its single gesture: the ever-dividing cell'.[3]

gael newton

references

1. *Gordon Bennett, letter to Christopher Chapman, 6 April 1994.* **2.** *Ibid.* **3.** Ian McLean, 'Psycho(d)rama Mirror Line. Reading Gordon Bennett's Installation Mirrorama', *Third Text, No. 25, Winter 1993-94, pp. 89–90.*

The uniform in *L.A.P.D. uniform* is vastly oversized, and yet the scale is carefully calculated. It is much too big to be simply the largest commercially produced fitting, and this implicity distances it from the aesthetic of the readymade. Like many of Burden's other object pieces, this work has a craft-discipline which relates it to the aesthetic, or indeed the ethic of the performance pieces. The ultimate futility of such meticulous reproduction (whereas mimesis is always translation) has obvious affinities with the extreme but absurd actions for which Burden first became well known.

Enormous as the uniform is, it is not quite beyond the bounds of conceivable human scale. Although empty, it can still evoke the potential of terror, and this impassivity, this silence which leaves the viewer to reflect, can better evoke the ugly associations of the Los Angeles police force than any overt denunciation. Like Timanthes the ancient painter, who veiled the face of Agamemnon because he could not represent his grief, Burden has chosen a 'negative way' in a world anaesthetised by hysterical overstatement.

Both the evocation of violence and the use of the negative way are themes of long standing in Burden's work. In his most notorious performance, he was shot in the arm by an assistant; but this piece has a sensational

quality that is finally less impressive than some that are not so generally familiar. For his graduation work as an art student, Burden had himself shut up in a locker, crouching in foetal position, for three days. In a later work, he lay on a ledge in a gallery for three weeks without coming down; and in another case sat on a chair on a dais for forty-three hours until he fell off. Unlike some performance works involving pain or mutilation, Burden's pieces have typically avoided anything theatrical and above-all illusionistic. When the performance was to lie on a shelf in a gallery, there was no question of going home when the gallery closed. If illusion is the production of appearance where there is no reality, Burden's concern is the opposite; his dedication to the reality of what he does is such that he has sometimes seemed uneasy about letting it appear at all: some of his performances have had very few witnesses, and the ledge in the gallery was so designed that the performer remained invisible.

Burden's work grows out of the end of the American abstraction which briefly dominated the world of postwar art. Abstract Expressionism made a cult of the artist's creative gesture, of the wellspring of creation and originality within the individual from which art was held to emerge. This emphasis on the individual and the subjective was a natural reaction to a

world in which the active co-subjectivity of community had been replaced by the mere aggregation of fragmented humanity: the *common* had given way to the *mass*. But was the isolated individual capable of providing a way to the whole? And in any case, the expressions of the pure subject all too soon became saleable objects on the art market.

Burden's performance pieces belong to a movement of reaction against the commodification of authenticity, but they have a seriousness and intensity which set them apart from many other historically or generically related works. Like the Abstract Expressionists, Burden was in pursuit of the source and indeed the subject of artistic creation, but he was suspicious of a process of creation which had for its outcome marketable objects; and still more fundamentally, doubted the very possibility of giving objective form to what remained of authentic experience. Hence his adoption of a negative way.

It is as though, in express denial of 'Action Painting', the artist could no longer act at all. But he could still suffer. There is a certain affirmation, a certain sense at once of self-possession and of involvement with the world,

to be found through deliberate endurance of the extreme. But again, Burden has generally avoided theatrical displays of suffering; for such staging reduces even endurance to spectacle. One of the most characteristic aspects of Burden's performances has been their elusiveness: not only has he chosen apparently 'endless' events, like lying in a bed, but time and again he has kept some of the rules to himself, or concealed the point at which the performance started and finished. Sitting on a chair until he fell off was such an instance of elusiveness. After the interminable immobility, there was an event, but it was an event determined purely passively. And was it an intrinsically important moment — or merely a sign of the reality of the previous stillness? At any rate, these performances were not spectacles to be watched, but objects of meditation; which is why they can still be 'experienced' in Burden's catalogues. There is much in his work that recalls ascetic spiritual practices, and the theological associations of the 'negative way' are not out of place.

The performances ended as it became clear that nothing was too shocking or even boring to be welcomed by the bureaucrats of contemporary art. It was not only paintings that could be commodified.

Once again, many artists have tried to protest against the museumification of their work, mostly with a notable lack of success. Burden has done rather better with, for example, an enormous jack called Samson that was braced against the walls of a gallery and given a turn by every visitor to come through the turnstile. Less obviously, other more recent works with technological or military themes seem to resist the neutralisation of the museum milieu by affirming their involvement in concerns outside the privileged domain of the cultural. At the same time, like the performances, they are clearly something the artist does primarily for his own survival.

The police uniform too is at once a reflection on the social environment and an observation about cultural institutions. Distantly, it recalls suits of armour in museums; but here there are no romantic associations and there is no pleasing sense of the past. The uniform stands for power without authority, the predicament of contemporary culture. And displayed as an artwork it hints that contemporary art and its functionaries too rule by a kind of terror where there is no basis for shared understanding or dialogue.

christopher allen

CHRIS BURDEN

chris burden *L.A.P.D. uniform*, 1993–94 220.0 x 180.0 cm cloth, metal, plastic, leather, wood Created in collaboration with the Fabric Workshop/Museum during Chris Burden's residency. 1992–93. Courtesy Gagosian Gallery, New York

... 'blobs of glup' ...

hany armanious *Snake oil # 25-38*. 1994 hot melt, oil paint, MDF board, steel rod 120.0 x 240.0 x 120.0 cm. National Gallery of Australia. Purchased 1994. Courtesy Sarah Cottier Gallery, Sydney, Photo Ashley Barber

HANY ARMANIOUS

The snake which D.H. Lawrence encountered at a watertrough in Sicily was 'earth-brown, earth-golden, from the burning bowels of the earth'. It appeared 'like a king in exile, uncrowned in the underworld' but the writer threw a log at it, thus missing his chance with 'one of the Lords of Life'. Coming to terms with the mythic in nature is a standard Romantic theme, but in this century mythic qualities have also been divined in the industrially-produced objects which surround us in daily life. De Chirico's insistence in his paintings on the mythic/expendable — a rubber glove, biscuits, the red zebra from a liqueur ad — provided a necessary complement to the deadpan readymades of Duchamp. Nor were these items selected for their conventional beauty — the mythic endows its objects with something more than that.

It has been the inspiration of Hany Armanious to select items from his surroundings — often objects that we regard as rubbish — which are particularly *telling*, in the manner of dream narratives. By selecting and recontextualising a diverse range of cultural jetsam, simultaneously humorous and ominous, he has contrived a series of visual equivalents to the aphorisms of a holy fool.

The *Snake oil* works present us with more of these paradoxes — a vision of matter which oscillates between the priceless and the worthless — 'blobs of glup' set between the Seen and the Unseen. The juxtaposition of cast and morphic pieces further confounds our categories of natural and artificial. A sense of the subterranean pervades the work as a whole, as if the elements were stalagmites and uncut crystals brought back from caverns (measureless to man and guarded by serpents) for commercial display. The distinctions between industrial and psychic *objets trouvés* have been eroded.

One of the more telling historical narratives concerning alchemy is that of the seventeenth-century physician Helvetius who met a stranger who offered him a sample of the materio-spiritual, gold-producing philosopher's stone. Helvetius complained that the piece was too small, to which the stranger responded by 'cutting halfe off with his nail' and giving back the remainder, saying 'It is yet sufficient for thee'.

Armanious's 'sufficient' is in the form of more (rather than less) than enough. His material, hot melt, is transformed by a series of alchemically suggestive processes from something akin to industrial waste into works of high art. The shimmer on their surfaces is an authentic index of their value and we are in the presence of an Arabian Nights display of fabulous, impossible wealth.

judith pascal

Waves Generated by Damien Hirst Thousands of Miles Away Breaking on a Reef in My Head

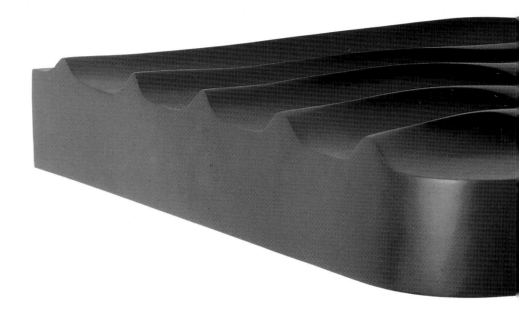

ASHLEY BICKERTON

Ashley Bickerton's *Waves generated by Damien Hirst thousands of miles away breaking on a reef in my head* 1993 is a black shelf-like fibreglass form that floats out from the gallery wall into the viewer's space. With a semi-circular opening in its front edge and seductive curling waveforms on its upper surface it could be a prototype for a virtual reality helmet custom designed by a surfer. Its matte black surfaces are imbued with a curious mixture of psychological interiority and menacing appearance. An appropriate combination: for, as any surfer knows, a reef can be a dangerous place; it is also where you can catch the biggest waves. Of any of Bickerton's peers, Hirst generates some very big waves, not just in terms of public profile but in terms of the psychological buttons pushed by his work. Life and death, fascination and fear are Hirst's touchstones, but they have also long been close to the heart of Bickerton's own practice.

Bickerton's signature constructions of the mid–1980s invoked a curious sense of dread. Large boxes or containers padded in vinyl and emblazoned with logos, representing art world subjects as fashionable commodities, were hung from immaculate oversized brackets and cantilevered aggressively off the wall. Curiously, the work also seemed precarious, as if its aggressive thrust and all that protective gear was just a façade to ensure that you kept your distance. Its protective padding and fetishised hardware also gave the impression that this was work that was built to travel and would never rest for long in one location.

His eco-sculptures of the later 1980s also managed to seem simultaneously threatening and threatened. Containers of material (natural and cultural) variously padded, strapped, suspended and protected, functioned metaphorically as biospheres and for the role that human influence plays in them. In this, Robert Smithson's site/non-site works — installations of metal containers filled with mineral samples, maps, photographs, and drawings all taken from an industrial site — are an important touchstone. Just as Smithson's work proposed a kind of non-mimetic equivalence between the industrial site and its displaced referent in the gallery, Bickerton's eco-sculptures stood in for the environmentally threatened landscape. In many of these works natural and cultural materials are contained side by side. The fact that it is usually the environmentally toxic cultural materials that appear far more

seductive hints at the difficulty of shifting our mind set, however important the predicament. Far from intending this as an ironic gesture, Bickerton asserts that 'it is precisely the exchange between the anthroposphere and the biosphere that has become central to the work. It is in this overlap I desire to create the bleakest and most hopeless art.'[1]

Many of Damien Hirst's works are also bleak self-contained systems, standing in for human social relations. His *One thousand years* is a vitrine, divided in two, containing hatching maggots and sugar water on one side and a skinned cow head and fly zapper on the other. As the maggots mature into flies they can fly through holes to reach the cow head and the fly zapper, whereupon a carnival of life and death is played out before our very eyes. The flies find the cow head to feed and reproduce or they are seduced and killed by the fly zapper. Whether this is a *tableau vivante* or a *nature morte* depends entirely on your perspective.

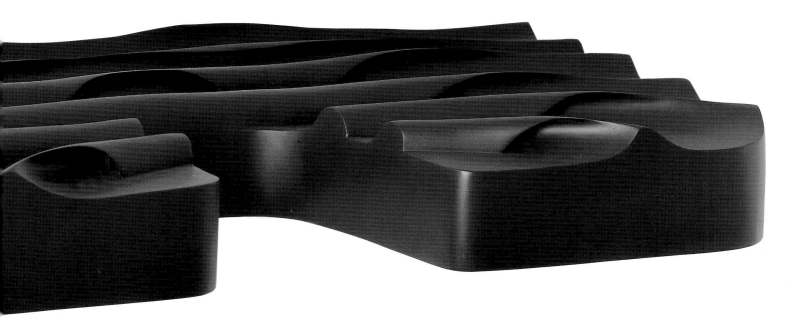

The title of *Waves generated by Damien Hirst thousands of miles away breaking on a reef in my head* connects it to the art world self-referentiality of Bickerton's constructions of the mid-1980s, but this time it serves a very different purpose. Where his earlier work seemed to be commenting on the commodity structure of the art world and its star system, a recent quote would indicate that he has long since found this position highly limited: 'A friend Mark Dion once said something that stuck with me; "Move your art choices as close as possible to your lifestyle choices." To this I will add, "Make your lifestyle choices wander far from the feeding trough of our art ghetto".'[2] In the case of *Waves generated by Damien Hirst thousands of miles away breaking on a reef in my head*,

Bickerton is not simply referring to Hirst as an art star or a product; rather he appears to be referred to as a practical exemplar. Through aesthetic means, his art poses questions about the nature of life, not simply propositions about art. Not that Bickerton's work has ever been in danger of being too cosy in the virtual space of the art gallery either; the consistent references to social and ecological issues made sure that one always remained keenly aware of the world beyond the gallery walls.

Bickerton's most recent work seems to continue his practice of exploring the links between physically and

conceptually disparate sites, while giving form to the psychological states generated by those increasingly inevitable links. His peripatetic lifestyle is an important source for much of this work. Recently he commented that, 'I have seen a certain bad New Jersey haircut everywhere that I have been. I cannot help thinking that a bad New Jersey haircut can travel faster and with more precision than all our best intentions. In terms of the millennia of unchanging human involvement on the planet, it is bizarre that it only takes a microsecond to crawl out of a dim Stone Age past and straight into a grubby Batman T-shirt, one of the farthest ranging missionaries of the new "soft" imperialism.'[3] *Waves generated by Damien Hirst thousands of miles*

away breaking on a reef in my head is a reminder of the way in which cultural experiences are transmitted across vast geographical distances within the space of a mind. It is a reminder that at this point in history the possibility of pure interiority is as much of a fantasy as is a site of uncontaminated nature. Bickerton seems both wary and gleeful of this state of affairs; mindful of the dangers of homogenisation and gleeful at the possibilities of miscegenation. Any hope that the next wave will carry us out of our various predicaments is endlessly deferred in the knowledge that there is always another wave on the horizon.

trevor smith

references

1. Ashley Bickerton, 'Une Conversation avec Marc Dion', Galleries, October/November 1989, p.149.
2. Ashley Bickerton, '"Just Another Shitty Day in paradise!" (A Travelogue)', artist's statement, The Contemporary Arts Centre, Cincinnati, Ohio, 1993. **3.** Ashley Bickerton, Documents, p.64.

UNITED COLORS
OF BENETTON.

REAL RELICS LYING: ANTONY HAMILTON

MISS OR MYTH? was a banner headline for a front page story datelined 'Eucla: Today' in the *News*, 'Last [edition] Adelaide: Friday, December 31, 1971/Very Happy/NEW YEAR/To all our readers'. An afternoon tabloid, now extinct, the *News* was not primarily for news. Its true self flowered in the marvellous headline for the summer-holiday, slow-news 'silly season'. ❖ That MISS OR MYTH? of midsummer 1971–72 was the Nullarbor Nymph. On Christmas Eve she was created, over a beer or two at the Amber Motor Hotel at Eucla, by a travelling publicity agent and two local bushmen — she was specifically for press consumption. TV and radio did not then reach the remote place 1500km from Perth and Adelaide, but the papers did, and their ways still structured Euclan thinking. First reported on Boxing Day, it was a 'Tarzan Girl' that trappers had seen, then a 'Nature Girl'. After a few more days of collective work in the bar, she became the Nullarbor Nymph, and for the New Year she materialised in a photograph splashed through the press. ❖ Antony Hamilton's MISS OR MYTH? completed in midsummer 1993–94 is a floor and wall installation which presents a few traces of the nymph, found or fabricated by the sculptor. He first reconnoitred the Nullarbor Plain's western end in spring 1992 and scavenged roo-shooters' and rabbiters' sites. Gestation was slow and steady, but on a summer visit in December 1993 he made an exciting find. It short-circuited the process of art-making and the completed work was ready for exhibition in January 1994, at the Anima Gallery, Adelaide. There it was contextualised not only by the artist's biography and a complex descriptive label, which we will come to later, but also by colour snapshots of two tan-coloured holes in the Plain (Woodella Rockhole holding surface rainwater, and Weebubbie Road Blowhole which alternately sucks in warmth at night and puffs out cool underground air into the day), and copies of pages from the *News*. ❖ NATURE GIRL'S HIDEOUT FOUND was a pre-nymph report — nicely circumstantial but in fact from a fictional 'Eucla bushman Mr Dougal Kingsbury' — of 'the Nullarbor nature woman, the blonde girl seen running through dense bush and hand-feeding giant Red kangaroos ... A cave containing the remains of an old mattress ... The floor of the cave contained human footprints and outside the tracks of kangaroos were everywhere. One set of roo pad prints were of a roo which must have been a good 8 feet tall, Kingsbury said ... When he found the cave the roos stood about 100 yards away and watched him. He said it was a most odd feeling and made him believe the Nullarbor nature woman was in the cave. He did not see her.' Then followed: 'MISS OR MYTH?' with its continuation, 'Nymph Hunt' and 'IS THAT NULLARBOR NYMPH/A HIMPH?': 'An Englishman went missing ... With his hair grown long he could have been mistaken for a near-naked girl.' ❖ The fictional bushman Dougal Kingsbury faded away in favour of genuine 'Eucla bushman and rabbit trapper', Ron Sells. He was the first claimant of sightings, and the most convinced. 'We first heard of this woman living with kangaroos nine months ago, and thought it was a bit of a joke. But last Thursday [the day before Christmas Eve] I was out setting traps 15 miles north-west when I noted 15 or 20 roos. I thought I'd shoot one for dog meat when I saw this girl. She was pretty well stripped down, just a short skirt of skins and long blonde hair half-way down her back. She's about 5 feet 8 inches tall and, judging by her figure, I'd say in her early 20s. She took off into the scrub and I tried to chase her in my old Morris but we hit a stump and I shattered the sump. On Monday just before sundown with a few blokes aboard an old Land Rover, we saw her with about 10 roos only about 7 miles from town ... We called out but she took off again and it took us about half an hour to get the old bomb going so we lost her.' ❖ At thirty-one Sells was the youngest of the 'middle-aged' men about Eucla who created the nymph and he was the most photogenic. He was an Aussie amongst the Germans and Scots and Lithuanians; his bushman accomplice Laurie Scott had recently abandoned roo-shooting for sharking, so Ron was the only hunter — in real bush clothing and an Akubra hat. There seemed to be a delicacy of feeling among the skylarking bush mates, hotel guests and pressmen that 'Sellsie' was the right mate to meet their nymph, the best match aesthetically and sexually. ❖ On New Year's Eve Geneice Brooker Scott (wife Laurie Scott) was filmed in colour on super-8, 'near-naked' in a Western Grey kangaroo skin lap-lap — a simulation of the nymph 'running wild and free', not with 8-foot Red kangaroos but with smaller Western Greys. Hermann Jonas, a guest at the Amber, made that film and the blurry black and white which became the canonical image of the nymph. ❖ Three words stand out in the making of the myth: nymphs, Nullarbor and Eucla. ❖ According to *Lemprière's Classical Dictionary*, 1788, nymphs were 'Certain female deities among the ancients ... Their residence [was fixed] in the sea, mountains, rocks, in woods or caverns, and their grottos were beautified ... They were generally represented as young and beautiful virgins, veiled up to the middle ... It was deemed unfortunate to see them naked and such sight was generally attended by delirium ...' ❖ Nullarbor is not an Aboriginal name despite its indigenous sound. It is neo-classical, from the Latin *nullus arbor*, and the right setting for a classical deity. ❖ Eucla is an Aboriginal name. Daisy Bates lived there once and said that *yerkla* or *yer coloya*, meaning 'bright fire', was the local name for the planet which Europeans named after Venus, the ancient Roman goddess of love. Whitefella Eucla was, however, the place where Australia became a primitive cyberspace. On 8 December 1877, Eucla's new telegraph station first repeated a telegram en route from Adelaide to Perth. Eastern Australia was already linked through the Adelaide–Darwin Overland Telegraph to Asia and Europe; now mechanical codes and electrical pulses, keyed into a wire, gathered Australia into a single conversational space; and for 50 years Eucla was, outside the State capitals, Australia's busiest telecommunications centre. ❖ In 1971 the Nullarbor Nymph's publicity man gave Eucla's diminished population as 'eight humans, four crossbreed dogs and an aged parrot that swears like a bushman'. New Eucla was posing as picturesquely regressed, rough and wild, ready for its motorist future on Australia's only transcontinental highway. The new Amber Motor Hotel was a goldmine petrol-beer-sleeping stop. ❖ On the 129th meridian of longitude, the border between the States, now stands a Big Kangaroo. Perhaps it reasserts indigenous, pre-Christian animist or nymphic culture over the 'Pope's Line', for along this very meridian in 1494, for orderly regulation of Christian missionary work and European colonisation, a Papal Bull, and then a bilateral treaty between Portugal and Spain, divided the world in half. ❖ The Nullarbor was the end of the European world. In an early expansionary phase the Dutch navigator Pieter Nuyts in 1627 ventured a bit beyond the Pope's Line, as far as present-day Ceduna, where Jonathan Swift's *Gulliver's Travels* — a science fiction for its day — placed the little people's island of Lilliput. Nobody from Europe visited again until British colonial times. ❖ The Nullarbor Nymph; Maslin's Beach — open near Adelaide for nude bathing; the Tidal Wave panic — a deluge feared for Adelaide, a city on a low-lying plain: those were the three things young Antony Hamilton already knew about his new State when in 1975 he found himself heading from a sheep-country childhood at Euroa, Victoria, to Adelaide's South Australian School of Art. ❖ Antony Chisholm Hamilton's family in earlier generations had known the painter Sydney Long and he knew Long's Austro-Classical mythologising: *The Spirit of the Plains*, naked freedom, a white girl dancing with brolgas; *The music lesson*, an Aboriginal nymph piping to magpies; *Pan* among the gum trees; a moon star goddess drawn to earth at '... *Twilight in a land of reeds'*. Straight out of art school, Hamilton in 1979 spent three months working the bowsers at Nullarbor Roadhouse at the beginning of the Plain. 'It was a mystic, animistic place. The land breathed and dimpled and sweated with its blowholes, sinkholes and surface-water rockholes. And the shrunken vegetation: I suddenly felt like a giant, or like Gulliver in Lilliput. The dingoes feel the same, they jerk up on their hind legs for standing views across the dwarfish saltbush.' That's a very Virtual Reality feeling. Inside a VR helmet-mask there are jerky changes in scale or direction: floating down a blood vessel for medical research, hovering above a city to plan new urban-design projects, or entering a Kangarassic Park for sci-fi entertainment thrills. ❖ The outback has absorbed Hamilton. He now lives at Beltana, a ghost town once the centre of camel breeding for desert transport. He wears R.M. Williams bush clothes and has grown a Burke & Wills beard. He is still and silent and watchful. He lived his art on long, slow camel treks before making a 1989 installation sculpture which explored another popular-culture media sensation. His partly readymade title was *I can only look out, like Mr Micawber, 'for something to turn up'. A view of the melancholy situation of the party Burke, Wills and King of the Victorian Exploring Expedition of 1860*. Not far beyond Hamilton's Flinders Ranges base, Burke and Wills died from starvation, unable to break out of their European virtual reality. In the real reality of Aboriginal Cooper's Creek at Innamincka there was plentiful bush tucker. ❖ We can now consider the artist's complex label for his Nullarbor installation: *Antony Hamilton/MISS OR MYTH?/Sub Titles (Elements)/'Near-Eucla'/Old forty four gallon drum, surface water./'Diamond Ice'/Kangaroo shooters' ruined vehicle hood, beer bottles, natural light beam./'Spirit of the Plain'/Found dress (December 1993), attached portion of printed newsprint, old phone number on reverse, from pocket. Kangaroo doe skin, tanned with Eremophila Longifolia leaves and sewn with kangaroo tail sinew and human hair. Piece of kangaroo buck skin, tanned with Eremophila Longifolia leaves.* ❖ The floor elements are velvety rust-red, and mostly male. The 'Near Eucla' drum resonates with the nymph's wistfully repeated description 'near-naked'; it is a scrub signpost to Eucla, but it can be turned and is untrustworthy — its back says GO BACK; gunshot has pierced it and the bullet holes are spotlit; its top is a shallow dish for what the artist privately notes as 'Nature element (Rain)'. 'Diamond Ice' is the name of a bush-track junction and kangaroo chiller site, and it became Hamilton's name for the rusted white car hood which once marked the bush camp of Laurie Scott. The hood's sheltering cave form has become a fairy-nymph's bower, a grotto beautified with amber-brown Swan Brewery bottles, glistening. Soft light enters through a square hole which once housed a blinding roo-shooter's light; this is privately noted as 'Nature element (Light)'. Is it a killing ground? Was the hunt stilled by an allusive glimpse of nymphic mystery? Or was a hard gaze at nakedness attended by delirium?

---

antony hamilton MISS OR MYTH?/Sub Titles (Elements)/'Near Eucla'/Old forty four gallon drum, surface water./'Diamond Ice'/Kangaroo shooters' ruined vehicle hood, beer bottles, natural light beam./'Spirit of the Plain'/Found dress (December 1993), attached portion of printed newsprint, old phone number on reverse, from pocket. Kangaroo doe skin, tanned with Eremophila Longifolia leaves and sewn with kangaroo tail sinew and human hair. Piece of kangaroo buck skin, tanned with Eremophila Longifolia leaves.. *1994 installation at Anima Gallery, Adelaide, Photograph by Clayton Glen*

The wall-hung 'Spirit of the Plain' hovers above the floorpieces, not quite like hunters' trophies. This element is mostly female. A real polyester dress, perhaps a Golden Fleece waitress's uniform from Eucla, was found by Hamilton beside a blowhole on his second visit — the find caused him to abandon his copying, from a museum's collection, a kangaroo-skin dress made in a European design by Aboriginal women from a Lutheran mission. A readymade 'wild dress' from the bush was always going to be better than anything he could make, and it was *blue*. A doe (female) Red kangaroo usually has 'blue' grey fur — though the stiff lap-lap fashioned by Hamilton (his only fabrication) is from a doeskin which had red fur.

He conceals this, facing the fur inwards as a lining to caress the nymph's imagined skin, except that the skirtfront gapes erotically open and its plaited drawstring of blonde human hair hangs loose. Above the empty miniskirt is a buck Red kangaroo skin, red male fur facing out, not tailored into a garment but schematic of a shirt, or of a torso. Did she wear it as a bib to protect her breasts? Was she masquerading as an amber-chested male kangaroo? Or being raped?   ◆   The Nullarbor Nymph, dreamed into being by some Eucla bushmen, was beautiful in her freedom. Hamilton admires the dream of beauty but brings it, gently, down to earth — where decay has its natural beauty too. The creation of a cartoonish virtual reality myth is something to admire, but the necessary starting point was real reality.   ◆   Populist entertainment constantly tends away from reality, towards myth — to encompass dinosaurs, Stone-age man, pagan gods and gladiators, medieval knights and maidens. There are Spielberg's movies and TV soaps. Now they have been joined by the cartoonish re-creations in the cyberspace of keyboard-and-screen, and the similar style of embryonic glove-and-helmet VR entertainment.   ◆   The heading MISS OR MYTH? might not quite equal the Murdoch American press's HEADLESS MAN IN TOPLESS BAR or KILLER BEES HEADING SOUTH, but all carry the inventive Australian style so admired by American connoisseurs of tabloid popular culture. Antony Hamilton has run with the roo-girl of a past telexed, telephoned, halftone-pictured tabloid cyberspace. He has given her a boost into new minds and, maybe, into some future News Corp VR entertainment. But best for him is the loopback. His real things found in the real world have become rustic relics of a myth.   ◆   Good myths grow from marvellous, powerful specificities inherent in 'the different places of the earth and the various functions and occupations of mankind'. We are told that 'the number of the nymphs whose power extended [over these places and functions] was according to Hesiod above 3000'. Hesiod, a poet 'in the age of Homer ... lived in a bleak country district. He is the first who wrote a poem on agriculture ...', so he would be pleased the nymphs continue to increase, in the bleak country of the Nullarbor Plain, and in belated acknowledgement of roo-hunting as a function of mankind.

daniel thomas

acknowledgements

Geneice Brooker Scott and her hunter husband Laurie Scott, Ceduna. The nymph photographer Hermann Jonas, The Pines. The artists Antony Hamilton, Beltana, and Dora and John Dallwitz, Adelaide. The Eucla Motor Hotel (formerly Amber Motor Hotel, Eucla) owner Steve Patupis and his daughter Rasa Patupis. The Adelaide pressmen Ron Boland, Tony Baker, Murray Nicoll, Mike Jaensch, Michael Conry, Bert Stanbury, Bob Cunningham, Sam Cheshire, Peter Haran, Brian Webber. The Adelaide historians Geoff Speirs, John Tregenza, Wilfred Prest. Also Basil Fuller, *The Nullarbor Story,* Rigby: Adelaide, 1970. For photographs, Victoria Bowes, Martin Hughes and Andy Hall, the *Advertiser,* Adelaide.

(left to right) Hermann Jonas, Ron Sells, Siegfried Krause, Laurie Scott, at the Amber Motor Hotel, Eucla, 31 December 1971. Photograph Ian Coventry for the *News*. Courtesy the *Advertiser,* Adelaide

Ron Sells with the nymph's footprint, near Eucla. Photograph Ian Coventry for the *News*. Courtesy the *Advertiser,* Adelaide

ROBERT MACPHERSON

Robert MacPherson wrote about his use of re-cycled detritus *Relics of boredom — Sculpture* exhibited at Art Projects, Melbourne in June 1981:

The sculptures have been collected by me over a period of 3 years from the floors of the highrise office block where I work as a cleaner. I think of them as : relics of the need to touch / freehold — shape — mould — alter.../ create / thus they are finger — fingers — hand — hands.../ human scaled / relics of that tactile need / *the need to makes everyone an artist* [1]

There are eight grey army blankets each with a word or words stencilled on it in bold red:

WHITE LADY   BLUE LADY   GOOM   BUSH CHAMPAGNE   MONKEY'S BLOOD   MUSICAL MILK   WHITE ANGEL   STEAM

They are words *souvenired* from the language of methylated spirits drinkers.

White lady is metho. Blue lady is metho coloured with blue — it was put in during the 1950s and 60s to stop people drinking the stuff. Goom is an Aboriginal name for metho. Bush champagne is metho and alka seltzer. Monkey's blood is metho and port. Musical milk is metho and milk. White angel is metho and white shoe cleaner. Steam is metho. MacPherson has written:

[M]y milieu has taught me, as I've moved in and out of different strata of society; from base (or so-called base society) to so-called higher levels; that each level has its own jargon. The language used in the work is the specialised language of the 'derro', the 'vag', the 'plonko', the 'goomie', the 'alky'. This jargon I find beautiful, descriptive, rich, wonderful: metaphorically, it is poetry. [2]

He has also said: 'I see painting as an anachronism, a dying or dead form, dying under the weight of late twentieth-century image pollution. I see all painters as naive painters. My use of non art objects, objects often at the end of their development, at the end of their function, is a reflection of this view.' [3]

mary eagle

references

1. *Written statement by the artist, 1981. National Gallery of Australia Registry file.* **2.** *Written statement by the artist, 1994. National Gallery of Australia Registry file.* **3.** *Ibid.*

robert macpherson *White Angel: 8 Frog poems for Little Jock, Hollywood George, Tom Pepper, Percy the Punter and Wattie Funnel.* 1983–93 synthetic polymer paint on wool blankets each 148.0 x 170.0 cm. National Gallery of Australia. Purchased 1994

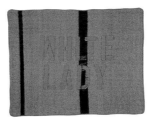

'You're driving like an idiot' He wobbled the steering wheel

We might ask what is the 'real' experience in Damien Hirst's passage of writing, in which our emotions are aroused by the experience of an horrific car accident; an ordeal that turns out

little, slowed down a touch and then speeded up, he got very clos

to be not actual. The car accident is a fiction within a fiction; an experience that comes across as first hand but is immediately shown as constructed by the imagination. We tell

to the car in front, dangerously close, flashed his lights. He looke

ourselves stories in order to make sense of our experiences — or, as Hirst would seem to suggest, we manufacture situations in order to experience what our lives mean. Damien Hirst

at his partner. 'Keep your eyes on the road,' she screamed. Th

has an appetite for images of death: his repertoire includes the student photograph of himself with the head of a corpse; a scenario of the savage and natural death of insects drawn to

car in front hesitated for a while to make a point, then indicate

bowls of sweet water only to be killed by a nearby bug zapper; and the brutal aftermath of murder in the blood soaked interior of *She wanted to find the most perfect form of flying* 1992.

and moved into the slower lane. (They ploughed into the back o

By comparison, as Gordon Burn suggests, *The acquired inability to escape* is the antithesis of those messy deaths. It is an image of death in life, anaesthetised and sterile. The larger

the car in front and span out of control, the bonnet clicked off it

section of the glass case contains an office chair, a clean office table, a lighter, a packet of cigarettes and a glass ashtray containing cigarette butts. The smaller section is empty.

hinges and ploughed through the windscreen and into th

Burn described the effect as 'atopian', 'no place', 'a sterile site ... simultaneously fortress and cage'.[2] As with a number of other works in *Virtual Reality*, the subject is human absence.

passengers. She moved towards the steel as fast, as it moved int

The situation may be likened to that proposed by Sartre; when, in looking for something, the absence of that something is the reality one lives. In Hirst's glass coffin, absence is

her, it was as simple as cutting white paper with scissors, bloo

overwhelmingly present. Glass as a substance is solid but invisible, in itself an image of palpable absence; through this material, simultaneously revelatory and resistant, we can see

spewed and pissed and spattered everywhere, flesh ripped. Th

everything but are unable to touch or smell. There appears to be no way into the work or escape out of it, only ideas can get in or out. The effect is whiplash, as in other works by Hirst.

dashboard cracked and scraped away her flesh exposing perfec

The table and chair set up an immediate possibility for most viewers (perhaps not bus conductors or farmers but almost everyone else, even school children) to imagine themselves the

shiny redness, glass shattered. The whole car crunched. Everythin

absent actor in a threateningly familiar scene. And in this scene, there is the ashtray. Damien Hirst has spoken about the significance the ashtray has for him: 'I love the way you have

exploded, it was timeless, it had a perfection, no time to feel horro

a beautiful home, the house as a composition, and then in the middle of it you have an ashtray which isolates this horror. It's so stylish, reducing this horror to a virtual pinpoint ...

or pain, no time to hear sounds, simple precise clear, it was s

Ashtrays are like holes in our everyday situation and these holes get smaller and smaller but never actually disappear.'[3] He sees the 'whole smoking thing' as 'like a mini lifecycle.'[4]

clear.) He accelerated again and lit a cigarette, smoked with on

The acquired inability to escape is yet another work in *Virtual Reality* that is redolent with nostalgia for something lost. An imaginative recapturing of a well-knit system that in reassuring

hand and drove with the other, he kept looking at her teasingl

experience would be replicated again and again from the simplest aspect of nature to the most complex scientific equation; a lost world that was once handled by humankind, by the

taking his eyes off the road. She closed her eyes and leaned bac

child with his glass container of tadpoles and the smoker quietly condoning his own death. samantha comte

far into the seat and said, 'Okay then, kill me.

damien hirst *The acquired inability to escape.* 1991 glass, steel, silicone, MDF table, chair, ashtray, lighter, cigarettes 213.0 x 305.0 x 213.0 cm. Private Collection. Courtesy Richard Salmon Ltd, London

DAMIEN HIRST

references

1. *Damien Hirst, 'Love Will Tear Us Apart'*, Flash Art Aperto '93 Emergency/Emergenza: XLV Biennale di Venezia, *Milan: Giancarlo Politi Editore, p.306.* **2.** *Gordon Burn, 'Damien Hirst',* Parkett, *No. 40/41, 1994, p.59.*
3. *Adrian Dannatt, 'Damien Hirst: Life's like this, then it stops',* Flash Art, *No. 169, March/April 1993, p.62.* **4.** *Ibid.*

matthÿs gerber Postcards 1994 postcards dimensions variable. Courtesy the artist and Sarah Cottier Gallery, Sydney, Photo Ashley Barber

VIR
TUAL
REAL
ITY

NATIONAL GALLERY OF AUSTRALIA
10 DECEMBER 1994 – 5 FEBRUARY 1995

BMW

The driver; the machine;

the road - not separate,

but one.

The style; the technology;

the emotion - pure parts

to the whole.

Experience the ultimate

driving machine.

Call Rolfe Classic to

test drive the new

3 series Coupe.

TOTALLY
INTER
ACTIVE

Rolfe Classic

22 Josephson St., Belconnen, A.C.T. Telephone: (06) 251 3333

3 - 5 Botany St., Phillip, A.C.T. Telephone: (06) 282 2455

DL 218   GREY 1026

thomas ruff *Portrait*. 1990 type-C photograph 210.0 x 165.0 cm. National Gallery of Australia. Purchased 1993

It is possible to record the historical physiognomic image of a whole generation and, with enough knowledge of physiognomy, to make that image speak in photographs.[1]

Thomas Ruff's *Portrait* series presents a young German middle class — a singular, affluent generation who live in Düsseldorf and are all colleagues and friends of the artist. Their portrayal is cool, deliberate and composed. Like scientific data, all inherent complexities and ambiguities are reduced through refinement and repetition of lighting, scale, tone, background and pose. It is a calculated suppression of expression and characterisation. In his investigation of a genre which traditionally promises to reveal inner characteristics such as personality, temperament and mood, Thomas Ruff has rendered the portrait mute.

An antecedent to the series, which has influenced Ruff and indeed many young photographers, is *Face of Our Time* (1929) a book of sixty portraits by fellow German photographer August Sander.[2] His studies of local farmers and tradesmen in the countryside of Westerwald were the beginning of an extensive personal program to document the German people which would have been, had he finished his work, a comprehensive survey entitled 'Man of the Twentieth Century'. The project was systematic and hierarchical, 'proceed[ing] from the earthbound man to the highest peak of civilisation'.[3] It was to be an authentic and dispassionate chronicle of the artist's own time. To achieve this Sander rejected the aestheticising, painterly effects of Pictorialist photography which typified the work of his contemporaries. Instead he utilised glossy-surfaced printing paper customarily used for technical photography so that every detail that came before his 'cool, unjudgemental eye' was made evident.[4] Furthermore, as the portraits were intended to be solely representative of types rather than individuals, Sander listed only the sitters' occupations, never their names. Author and psychiatrist Alfred Döblin noted in his introduction to *Face of Our Time* that: 'Seen from a certain distance, the differences [between the subjects] vanish, the individual ceases to exist, and the universality is all that remains.'[5]

Thomas Ruff's anonymous portraits are similarly presented — in sharp focus as neutral, objective documents of faces that epitomise a single generation. Nonetheless, because they are printed in seductive 'living colour' and are magnified to several times larger than life size, there is a temptation to extrapolate non-visual attributes such as the sitters' characters from the extant information. They could be fascinating as physiognomic studies but the images promise much more than they yield; for, while the verisimilitude of photography is emphasised, its information potential is limited. As a consequence these ostensibly conventional, though highly seductive portraits ultimately comment on the limitations of all portraits. They are façades in the most literal sense.

Their apparent artlessness mimics ID portraits in which individuals are presented, not as they perceive themselves, but by their superficial, official identities. Here it is not the personalities that are of interest but the physical veneer that simultaneously unites and separates them. The code is very familiar — each sitter is viewed rigidly, straight on at eye level, expressions are deadpan and only head and shoulders are included. The camera scrutinises the surface — every detail and imperfection is disclosed. The seriality and precision of Ruff's photographs further highlight this convergence of art, science and surveillance. They contrast with traditions of portraiture in which characterisation of the subject relies on codes of gesture, background, dress and expression to reflect the persona that the sitter, or indeed the artist, chooses to present.

The impact of Ruff's spectacular enlargements (which cannot be realised here in reproduction) is partly due to their transformative effect. In close-up, each face degenerates from a single, complete entity to a series of discontinuous planes and details. Skin, hair and fabric are seen as variants of colour and texture; facial features are expanded to geometric forms and lines. They invoke the enlarged scale of cinematic close-up which alternatively both enhances and blocks our reading of images. In this respect, Ruff's portraits correspond to the strategies of many contemporary artists who 'rather than simply returning to established conventions (of figurative art), are undertaking a radical reassessment of the body which coincides with changes in the social and technical environment'.[6] Their tactics are to isolate and expose the substances and functions of the body, as in the fragmented and reconfigured body parts that comprise Annette Messager's photographic installations, Robert Gober's sculptures of disembodied limbs, and the displaced and enlarged digestive and reproductive organs of Kiki Smith.[7] The works highlight the contingent nature of identity and reassess aspects of human physicality that are typically neglected

in considerations of subjectivity. However, Ruff's portraits also and enhanced materiality of details such as skin and hair scale and glossy, artificial surface of each photograph finally Ruff's portraits allow an enticing though slightly discomforting another human being's face, yet at the same time we are In some respects it approximates an aspect of contemporary face to face but interface through proxies such as computer museum — a site for synthetic observation and for which Ruff's of gallery spaces, Ruff's large and slick serial portraits command to be read. They are immodest — excessive in their scale and photographic object rather than its subject. The face of our idealised façade.

operate antithetically to these concerns: whereas the clarity define the faces with an almost palpable reality, the enlarged repudiate their corporeality. It is an appealing paradox that proximity where we can examine absolutely every detail of protected from the confrontation of a personal encounter. experience, mimicking situations in which we no longer liaise networks. Moreover, the condition is symptomatic of the portraits are most specifically conceived. In the yawning caverns the space in which they hang and demand some distance in order physically seductive — emphasising the pure presence of the time has been silenced to become no more than an

kate davidson

august sander *Zimmerleute (Travelling carpenters)*. 1928 gelatin silver photograph 23.4 x 15.4 cm. National Gallery of Australia. Purchased 1985

thomas ruff *Portrait.*. 1990 type-C photograph 210.0 x 165.0 cm. National Gallery of Australia. Purchased 1993

face of our time: the portraits of thomas ruff

references

1. *Translation of August Sander 'The Nature and Development of Photography', lecture for West-German Radio (WDR), Cologne, 1931 in Robert Kramer, August Sander.* Photographs of an Epoch, *New York: Aperture, 1980, p.40.* **2.** *August Sander,* Antlitz der Zeit (Face of Our Time) *Munich: Kurt Wolff/Transmere, 1929.* **3.** *Translation of Sander's preface to* Antlitz der Zeit *in Robert Kramer, August Sander, p.11.* **4.** *John von Hartz, Introduction, August Sander, New York: Aperture, 1977, p.8.* **5.** *Translation of Alfred Döblin's introduction to* Antlitz der Zeit *in ibid., p.9.* **6.** *Giancarlo Politi and Helena Kontova, (interview with Jeffrey Deitch) 'Post Human', Flash Art, No. 167, November/December 1992, p.68.* **7.** *These artists have been represented in recent exhibitions such as 'Post-Human' FAE Musée d'Art Contemporain, Pully/Lausanne,Switzerland, 1992 (and other European venues). 'Corporal Politics', MIT List Visual Arts Center, Cambridge, Mass., 1992–93.*

35

simon linke *Joseph Kosuth, December 1985.* 1991 oil on canvas 26.5 x 26.5 cm. Collection Galerie Ralph Wernicke, Stuttgart, Courtesy Lisson Gallery, London

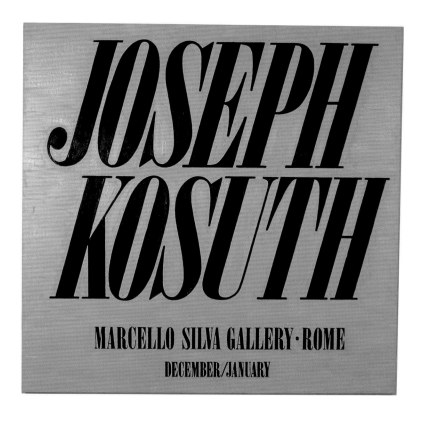

SIMON

It is well nigh impossible to create an artistic persona for Simon Linke based on his paintings. One cannot attribute any highly subjective motivations either to his choice of subject matter or to his treatment of it. From the act of painting and from the paintings themselves, Linke banishes the shamanism so often prized in the arts.

From the mid–1980s until the early 1990s the subjects Linke painted were advertisements from back issues of *Artforum*, the influential American arts magazine. His choice of individual 'images' was governed by a self-imposed logic: he went 'through an issue painting every page on which no editorial or photographic material appears',[1] thus denying the exigencies of personal taste.

This is not to say that Linke can be dismissed simply as a forger or a copyist. His pictures are clearly not facsimiles of *Artforum* advertisements. The differences mark them from the originals and introduce the possibility of other more subversive readings.

Linke paints the advertisements onto canvas rather than employing any form of mechanical reproduction. He also enlarges the originals, though still retaining the distinctive square format of *Artforum*'s pages. The physical, painterly qualities of Linke's pictures are conspicuous: James Roberts observes that the 'physical stuff of painting is present in abundance'; Jeffrey Deitch remarks on the 'sensuous, delicate application of the paint'; and Liam Gillick likens the paintings' surfaces to 'the cheesy painterliness of Mel Ramos or Wayne Thiebaud'.[2] In reproduction, the form in which they exist in *Virtual Reality*, the painterliness is diminished but remains apparent. It can be seen,

for example, in the fluctuation in surface density and in the wavering forms of some of the letters.

The alleged physicality of Linke's work does not result in an auratic effect. For, on close inspection, **the paint itself offers little of sustained visual interest. The only information given is the point the brush went on, where it went and the place it came off. A course describing nothing in particular, but the record of a disinterested filling-in of blank space ... The intense areas of activity in the paint surface around the letters seem somehow confused, as if they once had a purpose but have forgotten what it was they were doing.**[3]

The omnipresent brush marks are not expressive and do not shape images with meaning.

Linke's paintings present another conundrum. The *Artforum* advertisements offered information that was specific and could be easily understood. But, in translation, the clarity is lost. There is no correlation between the information value of the advertisements and the paintings of them: the exhibitions triumphantly announced in the advertisements are well and truly over.

This deliberate neutralisation of the original meanings of the advertisements has a number of desired results. It enables Linke to divorce his subject matter from any literal associations and, even more importantly, to render that subject matter 'meaningless'. The imagery Linke chooses to paint is basically irrelevant, it does not matter which artists, exhibitions or galleries are named.

simon linke *Richard Serra.* 1989 oil on canvas 182.8 x 182.8 cm. Private Collection USA. Courtesy Lisson Gallery, London, Photo Sue Ormerod

LINKE

By breaking the nexus between subject matter and meaning (as constructed in terms of traditional subjectivity), Linke pushes his paintings into another realm. It is one in which **the meaning of the work resides outside, in the wings as it were, where the powerful peripheral factors that formulate a reading come into play.**[4]

The meaning of Linke's work is not merely tied to context, it is created by it. To make sense of the work, therefore, the viewer must bring 'those outside elements to bear'.[5]

This brings us, once again, to Linke's selection of subject matter. The decision to use *Artforum* advertisements is clearly purposeful, even if the selection of individual images is not. *Artforum* advertisements (since replicated in a host of other international arts magazines) are at the pinnacle of arts advertising and have become an intrinsic part of what is now euphemistically termed 'the arts industry'. In these pared-down images, design and typography are dominant: just a few key words — the names of the artists and the galleries — are spelled out, their status verging on the iconic.

Linke's adoption of these 'culturally loaded'[6] images is not naive or accidental. It can be related to well-established traditions in the visual arts — the 'appropriation' of advertising imagery has a lineage spanning from Pop Art in the 1960s to Postmodernism in the 1980s. And it may well be part of a broader social critique — some have argued that Linke's paintings are an exposé of the power of advertising.[7] If the latter is true, it would encompass a certain irony. Simon Linke has created a signature style and a disinctive product with obvious appeal to the art market.

helen ennis

My thanks to Christopher Chapman for making available to me material on Simon Linke.

references

1. *Jeffrey Deitch, 'Abstract Advertising',* Simon Linke. *Tony Shafrazi Gallery, New York/Lisson Gallery, London, 1987, exhibition catalogue, unpaginated. Linke has also painted advertisements containing photographic images; his most recent works mimic the painterly gestures of the Abstract Expressionists.* **2.** *James Roberts 'Articulating Meaning',* Simon Linke, *Kohji Ogura Gallery, Nagoya, Japan/Lisson Gallery, London, 1989, exhibition catalogue, unpaginated; Jeffrey Deitch, 'Abstract Advertising'; and Liam Gillick, 'A funny thing happened on the way to* Artforum. *Simon Linke and the materialisation of the art advertisement', Artscribe, No. 87, Summer 1991, p.51.* **3.** *James Roberts, 'Articulating Meaning'.* **4.** *Ibid.* **5.** *Ibid.* **6.** *Jeffrey Deitch, 'Abstract Advertising'.* **7.** *Andrew Renton considers them in terms of a critique of painting, locating them within a tradition that goes back at least as far as Courbet, with Gerhard Richter as one of its contemporary protagonists. See his exhibition review, 'Simon Linke. Lisson Gallery'* Flash Art, *No. 152, May/June 1990, p.159.*

Simon Linke's paintings are included in this exhibition as catalogue reproductions only.

ETERNITY DESTINY FAITH WHITE ANGEL The words resonate, which is why they are emblazoned, large, on wall, canvasboard, paper and blanket. Before being chosen by an artist, the first and last words in the list were selected by a perfume maker and methylated-spirits drinkers respectively. Artists, too, have been charmed by their power of suggestion. **E** The words sparkle. In this context they are equal to each other and interchangeable, similar in proffering an ideal future and in the fact that their precise meanings are unimportant. Detached from their historic usage, though still trailing clouds of glory, they float in a promising ether. **E** On becoming commodities, the words were credited with an author or company name. **E** ETERNITY by Calvin Klein and by Sylvie Fleury DESTINY by Edward Ruscha FAITH by Imants Tillers and WHITE ANGEL by methylated-spirits drinkers and by Robert MacPherson **E** For Calvin Klein, ETERNITY is in uppercase lettering, plain, without serifs, white on grey in the advertisements, and more formidable on a square perfume bottle through which one observes the level of perfume going down, daily. And Fleury, who paints ETERNITY on a wall (to be shortly painted over), imitates Klein in everything except scale and context: the hand-made ETERNITY is in uppercase lettering, plain, without serifs, on a grey ground. DESTINY by Edward Ruscha and FAITH by Imants Tillers, independently of Calvin Klein, are similarly presented in uppercase lettering, neutral and white on airy grounds that echo the bland futurism of the words. Ruscha's bluish mist and Tillers's hand-prints have melancholy overtones of time and mortality — equivalent in what they represent to the changing level of perfume in the container and the temporary painting on the wall. **E** Of these futurist visions only MacPherson's WHITE ANGEL, stencilled in red on a grey woollen army blanket, flesh to the others' spirit, reports actual experience and projects a real future. **E** According to *Elle* magazine, ETERNITY is a perfume representing chastity, whereas the other recent, aphrodisiac perfumes, Poison and Obsession, represent the compulsion and danger of sex. So these perfumes in the age of AIDS are cued to attract attention. Are you the woman for ETERNITY or Obsession, for marriage or danger? **E** This, too, is the age of Attitude. Attitude is style without the expected cohesiveness of style. Instead it is ahistorical, unlocated, illogical, rhetorical, fictional, deliberately ungrounded, apolitical, imaginative, ephemeral. This style transgressing style refuses to acknowledge standards of evidence, reportage, and coherence, or even that such things exist. Attitudism's closest historical mate is late nineteenth-century Aestheticism. It is lifestyle, no less. **E** Sylvie Fleury is an artist with lots of attitude. She has exhibited the products we shop for — shoes, clothes and cosmetics by well-known makers — showing them in art galleries, at biennales, and deceptively in shop-windows and magazines. Unlike Jeff Koons, who represents consumer products by employing top craftsmen and scrupulously meeting the market's standards of craft and materials — claiming his role as artist not traditionally, as the maker, but like a filmstar posing as the model and the subject of art — Sylvie Fleury performs her role of artist through buying her art, like any shopper, and re-presenting it. She has exhibited dresses that imitate Mondrian's austere designs. She has abused the formality of modern art by methods suggestive of Lucio Fontana's slits. Primarily, however, she represents fashion. Is she therefore like Warhol? There is a Warhol-like type of involvement in what makes our consumer culture tick. But there are also unWarhol-like overtones of strategic criticism in Fleury's work: feminist positions, a questioning as well as an aping of artistry. She has explained her focus on fashion: 'It affects everyone, whether you follow it or react against.'[1] She claims to be 'nonrestrictive': not driven by theory or political correctness but by the ethic of shopping. She is led by her own preferences — liking synthetic fur for instance because it is 'used to make stuffed animals ("they are cuddly and sweet and a friend to advertisers")'[2]. She subscribes to creativity — 'whatever that means' — in so far as it is a matter of shopping well: *Creativity, whatever that means, is where you bring it, and how much you want to get involved. Using the right coin on the right jukebox on the right song can of course create the right mood.*[3] **E** She assesses art on a strict commercial basis. 'Desire calls for satisfaction. If it's not total some campaigns promise your money back ...'[4] (By contrast, the classic tough judgement of art is the test of time.)

E Fleury's wall-painting ETERNITY provokes matter-of-fact questions: with what right does she make her work? how is the object constituted? The frame of the word ETERNITY if painted on the wall of a shop would be advertisement, but in a museum the context is art — specifically the (by now traditional, much used) genre of the readymade. The readymade, an object already made, is brought into art purely through its exhibition as art. Because of its alternative existence outside art, it switches between art and its other context. In fact, that switch is its artistic content: there is always a duality, always the suspended philosophical question: 'with what right is the work made and how is it constituted?'. Nonetheless, there is in this work ETERNITY something extra to the philosophic switch of context. The correspondence between the hand-made wall painting and the advertising logo for a brand of perfume involves an awkward transcendence. Unlike the readymade, this word work by Sylvie Fleury has an artistic content — it is a painting with a poetic message,

sylvie fleury *Poison.* 1992 shopping bags with contents dimensions variable. Courtesy Postmasters Gallery, New York, Photo Tom Powel

sylvie fleury *Installation.* Galerie Gilbert Brownstone & Cie, Paris 1993

Eternity Destiny Faith and White Angel

and its perception as literature may occur quite independently of its readymade, surreal switch from life to art, from art to non-art. What happens to this experience — is it authentic? what would be its context? — when the viewer remembers the second frame: the perfume. **E** The questionable presence of ETERNITY in an art museum may be compared with an extraordinary frame. According to advice about the frames around paintings: 'A frame that is too present, too rich, or too eccentric, will disturb the framing more than would the absence of a visible frame.'[5] The exhibition *Virtual Reality*, if succeeding in its coalescence of art and shopping, does not provide a safe context for ETERNITY. Sylvie Fleury's work — as virus or parasite on the world's framing of it (art, fashion, literature and religion) — introduces disorder into communication. ETERNITY is capable of disrupting destination.

mary eagle

references

1. *Sylvie Fleury, quoted in Elizabeth Janus, 'Material Girl',* Artforum, *No. 30, May 1992, p.79.* **2.** *Ibid., p. 81.* **3.** *Interview with Helena Kontova,* Flash Art Aperto '93 Emergency/Emergenza: XLV Biennale di Venezia, *Milan: Giancarlo Politi Editore, 1993, p.284.* **4.** *Ibid.* **5.** *The sentence is quoted from an article about frames around works of art: Jean-Claude Lebensztejn, 'Starting out from the frame (vignettes)' in Peter Brunette and David Wills,* Deconstruction and the Visual Arts: Art, Media, Architecture, *New York: Cambridge University Press, 1994, p.118. Jacques Derrida has stated that when he looks at a work of art and asks how it is framed, he is looking for 'whatever in the work represents its force of resistance to philosophical authority, and to philosophical discourse on it ... yet I have always tried to do it by respecting the individual signature of [the artist]'. Peter Brunette and David Willis, 'The Spatial Arts: An Interview with Jacques Derrida', ibid., p. 10.*

WHY USE THE INTERNET?

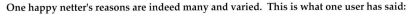

One happy netter's reasons are indeed many and varied. This is what one user has said:

"I think simply said the greatest benefit the net has been to me is that it was a valuable asset in helping me accumulate the knowledge necessary to change my career path. Up until three years ago I had never sat down at any computer let alone a PC.

Now I have both a DOS with Windows and a UNIX system at home. I have learned enough to program a dBase application for a local charity and am currently learning C++ and Perl. Also, I am running a private BBS for the friends I am learning C++ with and I can explain a bit about what the Internet is to people I know who have read of it.

Now how has the Net helped me here? Well the best I can do is give it in point form:

■ by subscribing to various lists, like com-priv, net-happenings and help-net I was able to get up to speed very quickly and am able to stay informed;

■ I ftp'ed Perl 4.0 from achive.cis.ohio-state.edu and installed it on my UNIX system;

■ I got help from comp.lang.perl and from comp.unix.questions;

■ I gophered to the O'Reilly & Associates site and ordered the two Perl books from them;

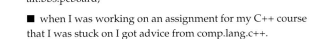

■ my local bookstore has said it would take six weeks to get them, I got them in three weeks and I live outside the U.S.;

■ when I was setting up the BBS I got advice from alt.bbs.pcboard;

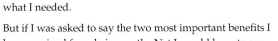
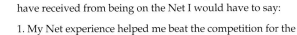

■ when I was working on an assignment for my C++ course that I was stuck on I got advice from comp.lang.c++.

There are many other ways that being on the Net has benefited me - for example when I couldn't find a recipe for a dinner we were going to have over the Christmas holidays I just did a Veronica search on recipes then on fondue and got what I needed.

But if I was asked to say the two most important benefits I have received from being on the Net I would have to say:

1. My Net experience helped me beat the competition for the job I just got with a local software firm; and

2. I have got a good friend from Poland through the Net. We "talk" on almost a daily basis. The Net has brought home to me what a small world we live in and that we are pretty much the same — no matter where we live."

To connect to the Internet in Australia contact: **AARNet**
Phone: 06 249 4969   Fax: 06 249 1369
email: admin@aarnet.edu.au
Postal Address: GPO Box 1142, Canberra, ACT, 2601

FAQ

Killing Others

Killing

DOOM

MAYBE WE'RE JUST BEING PESSIMISTIC

>rlogin DOOM 1:10pm Standard Mean Time ...

That slightly nauseating excited feeling starts to creep in as I boot up, logon to my account and the Net and start to scope around the BBs for DOOM players ...

mail message to: mandala@suburbia.apana.org.au subject of message: hey wnna play DOOM DEATHMATCH / :> copies to:

... invoking editor

Hey Mandala, TVI here, want to play? I'm logged on RIGHT NOW waiting to slay you yet again, so get your booty into action, mail me for conf. and we'll terminal download together. last one's a dead cybord! =:(Ps, nomonsters! mail sent !

... and so it starts, the typical e-mail message, cryptic DOOM terminology and the aggressive approach. This is DOOM, the three-dimensional, virtual reality type 'shoot-em-up' game that is sweeping the world in popularity and is rated as the most popular interactive game in the world at the moment. With bulletin boards dedicated to DOOMspeak, literally hundreds of thousands of personalised and customised versions posted throughout the Internet, plus the ability to play with multiple players (anywhere in the world via Internet) in real time, it is no wonder that id Software fully expect to be a major cause for decreased productivity in businesses around the world as more people play on-line from their work stations!

The features in this game are particularly noteworthy and there are some very interesting technical trade-offs which I will touch on presently. It is, however, the whole culture that has sprung up around this game that I wish to explore. There are questions to be asked here; there are some interesting stories about the game and its players and there is even the possibility for serious scientific research in the areas of psychology, com. sci. and virtual reality.

The user's ability to change radically the look and sound of the game opens up possibilities for experimentation with DOOM as an interesting medium with which to develop an artistic piece or performance. For example, students in the United States have been redesigning the DOOM environment to look like their own house or campus and even making the monsters look like their least favourite lecturers! Others have sampled sound collections from Star Wars and replaced the original DOOM ones so that when you use that big ugly chainsaw it sounds like Luke Skywalker's light sabre and when you die you hear 'Let the force be with you'. Is this versatility the reason why it is so popular?

Or is it the gore? The ability as in war to maim and kill the enemy — good against evil — in tantalising (tantalising in the context of the 'Attraction–Repulsion' theory) and varied ways, knowing that it is not real, certainly has its attractions. Or is the attraction the smooth gameplay with high speed and precision control on the user end, with high frame rate (the rate at which the graphics on-screen are updated per second) giving a smooth movement without the jerky motion so common in other 3-D games?

The trade-off is that speed and interactivity have higher priority than the visual accuracy of the environment — the texture mapping still leaves a fair bit to be desired and the enemy still looks like a cardboard cut-out with a modicum of artificial intelligence. The reason that the characters in the game look flat is because they are flat, in a computer graphics sense. They are just pictures mapped onto a polygon or two that have some animated properties, something like a puppet show consisting of moving bits of cardboard with a photo of Arnold Schwarzenegger (or whoever) stuck on the front. The designers have done this in order to avoid visual complexity. The update rate slows down proportionally as the number of polygons used increases (polygons are graphic building blocks for any 3-D environment), and ultimately the player loses a sense of real time interactivity. Notice, however, a clever little trick that has been employed in DOOM to create an illusion of substance: the characters are constantly facing the player — when one walks around a dead enemy the image always turns to face the player's viewpoint. It is flat but if one does not look too carefully the effect is a clever shortcut to visual complexity without slowing the gameplay down. Ironically, these flat, viewpoint following images are called 'sprites'. Other neat features include lighting tricks like strobing or diminishing of light: in the distance the light gradually gets darker giving an illusion of more space in the murky depths. Explosions light up adjacent areas and lights go on and off revealing glimpses of horror etc.

Technically it is all very exciting, but I'm not totally convinced that this is the sole reason for its enormous popularity.

The fact that one can play god by changing the environment is attractive and important. With the possibility of posting these augmented environments on the net for any number of the 27+ million users to play with, very interesting questions about the individual's influence on popular culture are raised. Sometimes these postings are anonymous. They even get rated for their ingenuity (like Top of the Pops) by publications such as the *DOOM FAQ*. The net seems to be free of restrictions over expression; anonymous works can be altered and 'evolved' with use. The potential for individual power is huge: anyone can have an effect and the amount of copyright free 'shareware' is enormous. Is the attraction the power of the individual to be the god, the artist, the doyen of her/his own personal environment? Is that all, or is it the fact that one can mess up that environment, that one has some control over it but not total control — you can still get killed remember (even if you've changed your enemy into images of gerberas) by the most violent means possible. Blood, guts and gore are firmly rooted in popular culture and because it's only a game, a sport, then surely we'll be able to differentiate between real and virtual?

I believe it is important to recognise where the triggers are being pulled in this game, just on the virtual BFG9000 (Big Fraggin' Gun) or the rocket launcher? Or are there some triggers inside us that are being squeezed? Perhaps one should also keep in mind that link between the virtual and the real: those cables that run from your computer to the modem sending electronic impulses throughout the net which come out at another modem through some more cables to another computer which is simply, elegantly and efficiently linked (via little cables) to a REAL BIG FRAGGIN' GUN or is it just a laser printer?

It is interesting to note that it would be easy to dress up the wolf in sheep's clothing and release DOOM under another guise as an exploratory interactive with simplistic role-playing components and some harmless looking obstacles that one has to throw softballs at to knock out of the way. But where is the fun and excitement in that? I want to kill and be killed, I want to be in extreme danger and I want to do it easily, smoothly, quickly and effectively with my friends in America, Ireland and Hong Kong and after dinner I want to play Death Hockey! (Death Hockey is one of the many user-invented versions of DOOM posted on the net. As the name suggests, this particular patch is a 'killer' version of the ever popular game of Hockey.)

christopher coe

acknowledgements

Mike Gigante, RMIT for advice and support.

The Total Immersion Virtual Reality Research and Performance Group, Melbourne for being a highly innovative bunch of people.

Martin Blackmore, Danny Gruber and Jonathon Zufi at the Virtual Reality Corporation, Melbourne for showing me their DOOM.

The Advanced Computer Graphics Centre, RMIT Melbourne for ongoing support.

Total immersion Direct to film digital image developed for the virtual environment performed at Scienceworks, Melbourne, November 1993

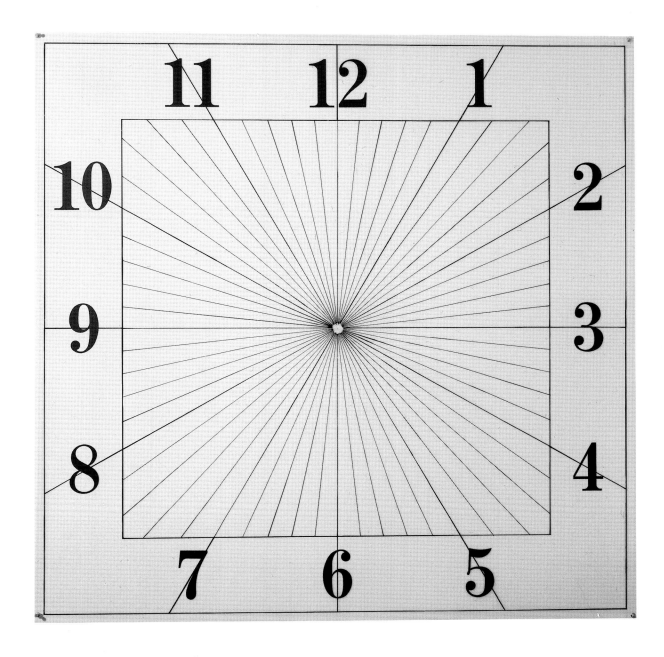

richard jackson *Working image for 5 Clock room*. 1994. Courtesy of the artist, Photo Josh White

reference

1. John Updike, Self-Consciousness, *New York: Alfred A. Knopf, 1989, p. 230.*

RICHARD
JACKSON   To stumble into Richard

Jackson's installation *5 Clocks* in *Virtual Reality* is an experience akin to that of
the shepherds in the painting by Nicolas Poussin who discover a gravestone with the
inscription 'Et in Arcadia ergo'. Even in Arcadia life ends, time passes. ● Time passes in Jackson's room:
it is a time machine. And like Dr Who's Tardis it is somehow bigger on the inside than its initial simplicity
indicates. Each of the walls, as well as the ceiling, is a clock with large moving hands charting the flow of time. The scale is
that of a tower-mounted public clock, but here the time is broadcast inwards, rather than outward, to focus on the visitor.
The space is cubic, a perfect chamber of reason — not a normal domestic space. The uniform dimensions of the floor and ceiling, even
with only one occupant, make the room subtly uncomfortable. ● Jackson's *5 Clocks* are dictatorial, they harass the viewer with their
pessimistic logic of inevitability. The longer they're looked at, the less time the viewer has left in their life. Surveys suggest that the average
time spent looking at a work of art in a gallery is just seven seconds. Seven seconds less of life for looking at each work in this exhibition, a rare
combination of pleasure and pain. But Jackson's *5 Clocks* perversely withholds metered satisfaction, as each clock in the room tells a different time. ●
Registering different times, the clocks convey the feeling of an international airport, with chronometers coordinated at the different global time zones.
Like this room of Jackson's, the airport lounge is a space in between places and in between times. Nowhere and somewhere: the clocks display future time
in one direction and past time in the other. In between times, Jackson's *5 Clocks* is a way station in life, 'time off' inside the clock itself to consider a personal
past, present and future. The notion of access to past, present and future in a single moment is reinforced by the differing times on each clock. ● The
differing registers also expose our conventional notions of time as a convenient fiction. The idea of ordered sequence is dear to us. Humanity's need to
measure and quantify finds its ultimate expression in the creation of devices to measure time, indeed the ambition to measure infinity is magnificent.
But almost unreasonably, in the face of such acute consciousness of time, there is a sensation of timelessness. ● In forcing an awareness of time in his
5 Clocks, Jackson generates a consciousness of life. 'Time, life, death, old subjects' said Jackson of this work, 'but it is interesting as I get older how my
perception of these subjects changes'. Time, broken into fixed intervals by the clock, is objective, but can be subjective when measured emotionally.
Time drags by when waiting for the bus, but 'flies when you're having fun'. Scientifically each day is 23 hours, 56 minutes and 4 seconds, but a
child's day is a long incident-filled learning experience when compared to the routine day of an adult. With age, days seem shorter, advancing
from the clarity of incident to a blur of motion. As Apollinaire wrote, 'Crowds rush toward death.' ● Time is at the centre of our
consciousness. Richard Jackson's *5 Clocks* attends to the human obsession with measuring, counting, mapping and inventing, coupling it
with the need to remove mystery from the world. Through such means we maintain a distance from life lest its brevity and
transience overcome us. In a digital or virtual world the process of sanitisation and distancing is near complete. Not only has
life disappeared, but so has death, replaced by a terrifyingly precise recording of populations, growth patterns,
property values. Jackson's time zone gently confronts these needs and fears, and offers solace. 'Existence
itself does not feel horrible', wrote American novelist John Updike, 'it feels like an ecstasy,
rather, which we only have to be still to experience.'[1] In the space between times
and between places, there is a moment in between the ticks of the
clock when time stands still. ● **michael**
desmond

It seems as if gut feeling is the only thing we can trust. The most appealing method of interpreting the world is based upon self-reliance and a trust in judgements that have no bearing upon the useless and trashy overload of information that constantly bombards us. Still, we cannot find solace in existentialism (it's seen as a pretence, and a masculinist one at that); and nature is neither pure nor sublime. Faith lies somewhere in our own personal experiences of the world; *and* although the notion of the universal unconscious is passé, it's through the memories and rehearsals of shared but differentiated experiences that we can assert our own sense of being. Everyone, it seems, lives in *their* own private Idaho, we each subscribe to *our* own personal Jesus.

Dale Frank's paintings — displayed in this exhibition as one of several components of his work — could be seen as an exemplification of this condition. Temporal in their execution and their resolution, the materials (the painting itself) will

Dale Frank and the Diamond Dogs

continue to slide across the surface of the canvas for the duration of the exhibition, and after. Frank's photographs and sculptures [1] evoke similar feelings — an ambivalence of such intensity, it typifies the sense of frightening doubt and unwavering faith

Cover, David Bowie's *Diamond Dogs* 1974, artwork by Guy Peelaert

that finds its zenith in adolescence. The residue that remains in our adult lives is rationalised but no less fervent. Our response to Frank's work (particularly some of his 3-D pieces) is a feeling of simultaneous anxiety and pleasure: the pleasure of recognition and participation; and anxiety induced by the work's empty spaces, the *something wrong* that washes over the object. What affects us is certainly what we add to the work, but it is also, to invoke Barthes, *'what is nonetheless already there'.*[2]

David Bowie's *Diamond Dogs* LP was released in May 1974, and took as its subject George Orwell's novel *1984*. Bowie had originally conceived a stage musical based on the book, however the trustees of the Orwell estate disallowed the project. Bowie's 1984 is a dystopia, a glittering ruins: 'fleas the size of rats sucked on rats the size of cats and ten thousand peoploids split into small tribes coveting the highest of the sterile skyscrapers'.[3] The track '1984' resonates with electric guitar chords reminiscent of Hendrix[4] overlaid with Bowie's haunting and exhilarating vocals; and 'Big Brother' still manages to surprise twenty years on with its mock-fascist chanting, vocal sampling and repetition.

That said, for Dale Frank to play this music over loudspeakers so that it resounds across the car park and entrance to the National Gallery is more a gesture of intervention than a commentary on Bowie's musical career. The ironies are still present in the lyrics, but in a sense (and this is also true of Frank's recent photographs) the content of the message is simultaneously relevant and beside the point. Frank's choice of music is predicated on his strategy of renegotiating the 'real'. The music is treated as a found object, but one that possesses very particular qualities. As is the case with his paintings, Frank confers

'a new *rhythm* upon a known image in a bid to modify its substance and meaning'.[5] Frank focuses on the palpable *effect* of the known object; his work explores the possibilities of our relation to and experience of this situation not only in art, but in contemporary life.

When American artist Bill Fontana fixed ten BOSE speakers to the façade of the Whitney Museum in New York, placing them at different heights to recreate the frequencies of the sound spectrum to mimic the height and sound of Niagara Falls,[6] he created a work that spoke not only of nature but of implications of audio verisimilitude. Frank's work, conversely, does not propose a dialogue about illusionism. Certainly the work opens up a space, but it is one that is aligned with (rather than at odds with) our experience of actuality. Listening to the Bowie music, the participant is immersed in a 'reality of fiction'. In this situation, as Eric Troncy suggests, 'the spectator is transformed into the *active actor*, carrying out and *finalising* a scenario that the artist has set up for him, ultimately modifying an instant of his behaviour'.[7] The point in this instance is the crush — there is no space between art and reality.

This is our experience of Frank's sound work: an ambivalence that typifies contemporary experience. We can assign probabilities but there will always exist a certain *degree of freedom*.[8]

christopher chapman

references

1. Dale Frank's photographs and sculptures, exhibited at the Canberra Contemporary Art Space, 10 December 1994 – 29 January 1995, as a component of the work at the National Gallery of Australia. **2.** Roland Barthes, Camera Lucida, London: Fontana, 1984, p.55. I am invoking Barthes's notion of the 'punctum' in photography. Opposed to the 'studium' (or what is represented), the punctum is the particular element of an image that is effective to the viewer ('that accident which pricks me (but also bruises me, is poignant to me'. p.27). The operation of the punctum in works such as Belanglo, Belanglo, Belanglo — The man who watches and touches from under chairs 1994 seems to override Barthes's subjective specificity. We seem to feel an effect akin to the punctum without a specific point of reference, we are moved or thrown by something simultaneously familiar and strange. The kombivan is identifiable and evokes a certain semiotic nostalgia, but its re-presentation by Frank adds a more insidious edge. Ultimately affecting the viewer is the overwhelming sense of aporia that is the basis of the object's attraction. This is the point where Frank's objects begin to intersect with the real world. They don't mimic or rehearse reality, they are. **3.** David Bowie, 'Future Legend', sleevenotes from Diamond Dogs, Chrysalis Records, 1974. **4.** Alan Parker played the guitar solo on '1984', a 'variation on the jagged, alarmist ack-ack guitar sound which Isaac Hayes derived from Jimi Hendrix and delineated as the principle motif for his soundtrack for the Shaft movie'. Roy Carr and Charles Shaar Murray, David Bowie, New York: Avon Books, 1981, p.64. Thanks to Ian Sharples and Suzy Saw for the Bowie material. **5.** Nicolas Bourriaud, 'Producing a Relation with the World', Flash Art Aperto '93 Emergency/Emergenza: XLV Biennale di Venezia, Milan: Giancarlo Politi Editore, 1993, p.39. Bourriaud suggests that the act of 'conferring a new rhythm upon a known image' is emblematic of the contemporary artist's relationship to the world. **6.** Bill Fontana's Vertical Water was a part of the 1991 Biennial Exhibition at the Whitney Museum of American Art, New York **7.** Eric Troncy, 'It's Alive!', Flash Art, No. 177, Summer 1994, p.107. Here Troncy is discussing a work by Felix Gonzalez-Torres, but the concept is applicable to Frank's Bowie piece. **8.** Brian Massumi, A User's Guide to Capitalism and Schizophrenia: Deviations from Deleuze and Guattari, Cambridge, Mass.: M.I.T. Press, 1992, p.63. Here Massumi invokes Deleuze and Guattari to discuss the consequence of the liquid (body) encountering 'noise' (disruption), and the resultant confusion, or openness of possible reactions.

Satellite Exhibition: DALE FRANK: SATELLITE OF LOVE

10 December 1994 – 29 January 1995
Canberra Contemporary Art Space
Gorman House, Ainslie Avenue, Braddon ACT 2601, Australia
12 noon – 4 pm Wednesday to Sunday

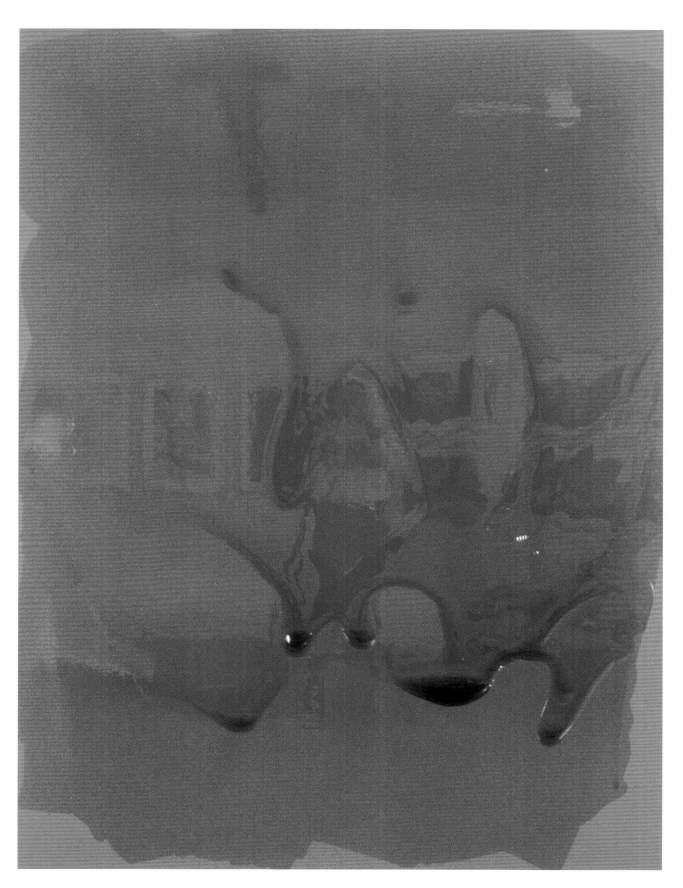

dale frank *The long
stunning death of the
great premature ejaculator —
swimming.* 1994 synthetic
polymer paint, varnish on
canvas 260.0 x 200.0 cm.
Courtesy of the artist and
Jack Shainman Gallery,
New York

VIR
TUAL
REAL
ITY

NATIONAL GALLERY OF AUSTRALIA
10 DECEMBER 1994 – 5 FEBRUARY 1995

I N D Y A T T H E G A L L E R Y

SiliconGraphics
Computer Systems

For more information please call: U.S.A. 1(800) 800-7441 Europe (41) 22-798.75.25 North Pacific (81) 3-5420.71.10 South Pacific (61) 2-879.95.00
Latin America 1(415) 390.46.37 Canada 1(905) 625-4747 Corporate Office: 2011 N. Shoreline Boulevard, Mountain View, CA 94043, (415) 960-1980.

And here I am already 'between heaven and earth', on the border. When I open my eyes slightly there is a pure, bright blueness, a radiant sky, the sea coastline is barely discernible in the bright fog below, a thin white strip of beach...[1]

ILYA KABAKOV'S SPACE

Ilya Kabakov experienced a sensation akin to that of flight, of being between 'heaven and earth' when he travelled unaccompanied around the Crimea, along an undeveloped coastline of the Black Sea. 'In a strange oblivion', Kabakov recalls, 'I stopped differentiating where the sky ends and the sea begins, where is up and where is down.'[2] *I will return on April 12*[3] is related intimately to this experience, the work seeks to express and induce a powerful sense of vertigo, of suggesting a situation (an experience) free of the constraints of a burdensome existence. A painting of the sky is placed on the floor. At one end stands a chair laid with a man's clothing, with shoes placed neatly beneath: it is, Kabakov suggests, 'the simple wardrobe of a person who has undressed and ...'[4]

It was first installed at the Goethe Institut in Osaka in 1989. The exhibition was to include kites, but as Kabakov states:

I wanted to make something that was contrary to everything else exhibited, along the lines of 'everyone has gone out to play but I stayed home', with all of the complexities of a failure, a person who has been left to sit in a corner.[5]

The failure is apparent. How is it possible to fly into a sky that is merely pigment on cloth, an impassable surface? Kabakov's work asks us to dismiss such pragmatic difficulties; the person whose clothes lie folded over the chair has, as Kabakov states 'gone with everyone'. *Everyone has flown into the sky, and so has he.*[6]

Like a pool, the sky is stretched out before us, recalling the fable of animals trying to catch the reflection of the moon in a pond, or, Kabakov suggests, 'the well known anecdote about the patients in an insane asylum who are diving into a pool

without water'.[7] Consider also the fact that astronauts train in tanks of water in order to experience a simulation of zero gravity.

Kabakov's experience on the banks of the Black Sea invokes philosophers Gilles Deleuze and Felix Guattari's description of smooth space:

... no line separates earth from sky, which are of the same substance; there is neither horizon nor background nor perspective nor limit nor outline nor form nor centre; there is no intermediary distance, or all distance is intermediary. Like Eskimo space.[8]

Deleuze and Guattari's smooth space positions itself politically — as opposed to striated or State space.[9] Smooth space relies upon the notion of flux, of an indeterminate and constantly shifting perception of volume and surface. A surface is less a membrane than a field.

For Kabakov, the act of diving into the sky is a political one. It embodies a gesture that challenges thresholds, reconfigures the world into smooth space, but like Yves Klein's *Leap into the void*, there is always an element of risk. The character in Kabakov's *The man who flew into space from his apartment* does so to escape complexities of oppression; the cramped physical space of the communal apartment in which he lives, the politics of a burdensome governmental system. The sky, ideally, is a neutral political and ideological space.

Kabakov shows us that the gesture of diving into the sky is a necessary act. More than a rehearsal of escapism, the gesture explicates truth, a brave idea, something *real*. And, as the artist has stated: 'the act of showing one simple real thing is revelatory'.[10]

christopher chapman

ilya kabakov *The man who flew into space from his apartment.* 1988 mixed media installation dimensions variable, as installed at Ronald Feldman Fine Arts, New York. Courtesy of the artist and Ronald Feldman Fine Arts, New York

yves klein *Leap into the void* as reproduced on the cover of Yves Klein's *Dimanche, 27 Novembre 1960* newspaper. National Gallery of Australia. Purchased 1983

references

1. *Ilya Kabakov on* I will return on April 12, *notes to the author, 1994.* **2.** *Kabakov, notes to the author, 1994. Kabakov continues: 'The second time I felt the same thing was when I was in Eric Bulatov's studio and I saw for the first time his finished work* I'm going! *which at the time seemed to me to be done with the same feeling that I have tried to talk about briefly here.'* **3.** *The date, the artist informs me, is of no particular consequence, ibid.* **4.** *Ibid.* **5.** *Ibid.* **6.** *Ibid.* **7.** *Ibid.* **8.** *Gilles Deleuze and Felix Guattari,* A Thousand Plateaus: Capitalism & Schizophrenia *(1980), trans. Brian Massumi, Minnesota: University of Minnesota Press, 1987, p.494. In note 28, p.574, the authors refer to Edmund Carpenter's description in* Eskimo *(Toronto: University of Toronto Press, 1964) of ice space and of the igloo: 'There is no middle distance, no perspective, no outline, nothing the eye can cling to except thousands of smoky plumes of snow ... a land without bottom or edge ... No flat static walls arrest the ear or eye ... and the eye can glance through here, past there.' (unpaginated)* **9.** *'State space is striated, or gridded. Movement in it is confined as by gravity to a horizontal plane, and limited by the order of that plane to preset paths between fixed and identifiable points.' Brian Massumi, introduction to Deleuze and Guattari,* A Thousand Plateaus, *p.xiii.* **10.** *Kabakov, 'Interview with Erik Bulatov and Ilya Kabakov, Moscow, July 1987, conducted by Claudia Jolles',* Erik Bulatov, *London: Parkett Publishers and ICA, 1989, p.44.*

As an artist Cindy Sherman makes photographs. Some three hundred of her works have been exhibited and published since 1976 — all untitled but individually numbered. The repertoire/modus operandi for which she has become renowned is the presenting of 'herself' in a seemingly never ending series of costume charades. The only consistently recognisable feature of Sherman's physiognomy is her hands — a part of the body resistant to make-up and make-overs. Mostly the images are presented in series; an awareness of the artist-in-disguise is thus intrinsic to the experience of her work.

Sherman states that the characters she constructs on her body are not autobiographical but reflections of ourselves.[1] Rather than submitting to a romantic notion that such recognition leaves space for a reinvention of the self,[2] the characters are a seductive demonstration that our 'selves' are symbiotic with a chaos of pre-programmed images. Sherman's images slip out from under simple categorisation — as narcissicism, self-portraiture or the self-promotion of media megastars, such as Madonna, with their penchant for presenting themselves costumed as multiple identities.

Sherman's 'characters' have all appeared before as stock-in-trade personae in film, television, fashion, advertising, pornography and high art masterpieces. There is no quest for authenticity as the mise-en-scéne is obviously constructed, clued principally by the lighting; objects are mere props. Her recent works, which no longer necessarily depend on the use of her own body, offer a mysterious fake-organic detritus with objects, dolls and medical dummies. The common denominator of her tableaux vivants is the presence of the overtly faked, and thus comes the realisation that in a media age we are more familiar with the reproduction than the original.

Nevertheless, there follows a certain compulsion to recover the original ideal-real image that compels this homage in Sherman's almost ritualistic tableaux. Recognition of any particular source, however, is academic; the images are beyond restitution as illustrations of some missing narrative.

Sherman's first body of work from 1975 is a series of small black and white photographs of herself in various locations and costume called *Untitled Film Stills*. They are not stills even from some imaginary film. At art school she had turned from painting to photography, as many of her generation would, feeling that painting was an exhausted medium. Conversely photography — the epitome of both ubiquitous replication and illusory snapshot truths — seemed to offer an appropriate medium for engagement with a fragmented late twentieth-century psyche.

For Sherman's generation the only truth in photography was that the camera always lies. By extension all forms of representation were lies. Only by pointing to the artifice of all imagery could there be even the possibility of integrity for the art work. This strategy of disputing the notion of authenticity involved a recognition that ambiguity was preferable to certainty. The second 'nature' of television, movies, magazines was their mother tongue. In the 1990s, identity is reconfigured as much as the eye in an age of virtual reality.[3]

In an essay on Sherman, Norman Bryson notes that the view which prevailed in post-modernist generations opposed the notion of the real to that of the copy; their notion of reality as a constructed spectacle meant that '[o]nce the world is declared to have become representation, and the real drops out of the system, the cultural sphere should be at peace, orbiting in the serene spaces of virtual reality'.[4]

Sherman's act of self-renewal by the 'morphing'[5] of a thousand image menus has been emblematic for a generation of artists emerging by the mid-1980s in Australia. The exotic work of artists such as Robyn Stacey, Tracey Moffatt and Anne Ferran suggests that such genres have appeal but no power if they can be mimicked so easily.[6] By manipulating the images of the past, they too have constructed clear careers for themselves out of ambiguity. Contemporaries of Sherman such as Australians Fiona Hall and Bill Henson[7] have consistently asserted the value and profundity of ambiguity, of living with uncertainty, of embracing the close encounters of fiction and reportage, elegance and corruption.

Sherman's works in this exhibition seem on one level to advance the cause of art and feminism not one iota! They come from a series commissioned by *Harper's Bazaar* in which Sherman was invited to photograph clothes from the new Spring 1993 collections. The images affront the fashion aesthetic of impossible perfection of form and lifestyle. Of the works, Sherman commented: 'I wanted to twist people's minds and then make them question their reactions.'[8] The figures are mere echo chambers of thousands of preceding images of the oriental siren and the classical odalisque. The translation is garbled and full of mixed metaphors; in *Untitled # 278* (John Galliano) the oriental is not svelte, feline or mysterious and slumps in a pose seemingly a parody of the pubescent figures of the painter Balthus. The chair in which she sits suggests both Louis XIV classicism and the leopard thrones of African potentates. Her white crumpled stockings recall the soft-porn exposure of Bellocq's photographic portraits of turn of the century prostitutes or the gross 'madames' so popular in twenties photojournalism. The bandages, cuts and torn stockings relocate the images to the reality that fitting the image comes at a price.

In *Untitled # 275* (Anna Sui) the classical odalisque, modelled on such images as Ingres's *La Grande Odalisque*, sprawls in a lurid eastern canopy. A welter of shimmering surfaces nearly cloaks her fake melon-like breasts tied on as once men wore codpieces. Such scale is unfashionable except in the limp narratives of pornography. Where Sherman's images usually arouse the viewer's curiosity about a missing narrative, here the evident boredom of the figures undermines the fictions.

These characters are enmeshed in the materials which shroud them and into which their patent corporeality threatens to dissolve — as indeed the corporeal does in Sherman's recent still-life images. In the late 1970s, pornographic magazines — owned by David Salle, a contemporary associate the artist — had acted as catalysts for her initial tableaux. Sexual representation is a theme to which the artist has given savage life through the 'sex pictures' in the 1990s in which medical dummies, porno plastic women, dolls and horror/sci-fi masks live an animated if feral existence — images also familiar in contemporary film and rock video/music.

The paradox of Sherman's work is that the images suggest that there is no originality — no identity — left in a world deluged by images, and yet her images are like nothing we've seen before.

gael newton

references

1. For a rare interview with Sherman see Gerald Marzorati, 'Imitation of Life', Artnews, Vol. 92, No. 7, September 1983, pp.78-87. **2.** A view argued by cultural critic Adrian Martin in his essay, 'Glamour the confession of a mask', in his Phantasms, Sydney: McPhee Gribble, 1994, pp. 100-107. **3.** See William J. Mitchell, The Reconfigured Eye: Visual Truth in the Post-Photographic Era, Cambridge, Mass.: M.I.T. Press, 1993. **4.** Norman Bryson, 'House of Wax', essay in Rosalind Krauss, Cindy Sherman 1974-1993, New York: Rizzoli International, 1993, p. 220. **5.** Term arising from film animation in which one form is transformed into another. **6.** The lure of glamour stereotypes for women artists has not been without problems. See Catriona Moore, 'Slave Girls: Welcome to the World of Style', SF Camerawork, Vol. 15, No. 1, Spring 1988, pp. 12–17, and Gael Newton, 'See the woman with red dress on ... and on ... and on ...', Art and Asia Pacific, Vol. 1, No. 2, April 1994, pp. 96–103. **7.** For Bill Henson see David Malouf (introduction) Bill Henson Photographs, Sydney: Picador, 1988, pp. 9–10 and for Fiona Hall see Kate Davidson, The Garden of Earthly Delights, exhibition catalogue, Canberra: National Gallery of Australia, 1993. **8.** Jim Lewis, 'The New Cindy Sherman Collection', Harper's Bazaar, May 1993, p. 186.

'i wanted to TWIST peoples minds...'

cindy sherman *Untitled # 275* (Anna Sui). 1993 type-C photograph 160.0 x 223.5 cm. Courtesy of the artist and Metro Pictures, New York

IMANTS TILLERS'S VIRTUAL REALITY

The presence of Imants Tillers's work in this exhibition undoubtedly is meant to make us think about its relationship to the contemporary machines of 'virtual reality': telephones, faxes, computers, up to and including, of course, the actual machines of 'virtual reality' now being invented. But, in fact, Tillers's work is not to be explained by such material phenomena, is neither their outcome nor equivalent. Rather, it would be what allows us to think about these developments, what makes them possible, how they might be otherwise. Art is always critical in this sense; it opens up a certain perspective onto things, it inhabits a different space from that of this world. If we can put it this way: it is that virtual reality which allows the 'virtual reality' of the world, that virtual reality which all those machines of 'virtual reality' try to stand in for and make real, but never finally could. Art is a kind of fictitious *doubling* of the world, much stronger than any attempt to realise it, to speak of it in terms of a real, whether 'virtual' or otherwise. It is art which is the true virtual reality and those machines which remain merely real — all too real. ✋ We see something like this in Tillers's own essay 'Locality Fails', still the best account we have of his work. He asks there whether an indigenous Australian art would be possible in a world that is becoming increasingly homogeneous, in which even the most far-flung parts of the globe are now being connected to each other by telecommunications. Such a regional art would be impossible, he argues, because we in Australia are so thoroughly saturated by technologies and images arriving from overseas. A provincial country like Australia is subjected to a constant flow of information from metropolitan centres like New York. As Tillers writes: **'Local' conditions might include the continuation of an Aboriginal presence in Australia, but equally they might include the transference of art information and models from New York to Sydney. For New York and Sydney are not 'space-like separated' at all: information is transmitted through identifiable channels (i.e., mechanical reproductions in aeroplanes) and thus arrives not mysteriously but by identifiable means.**[1] ✋ But Tillers also elaborates another, more mysterious 'failure of locality', this time proceeding not from the metropolis to the provinces but from the provinces to the metropolis. It operates not by 'identifiable channels' of communication, such as 'mechanical reproductions in aeroplanes', but by a kind of retrospective coincidence or chance. The example he provides of this, he admits, is 'almost preposterous', but it is, for all that, real. It is possible, he suggests, that: **[Arnold] Böcklin's painting *The Island of the Dead*, completed in 1880 in Munich, might be the direct (though slightly delayed) result of the successful extermination of the Tasmanian Aborigines by the white settlers despite the fact that Böcklin would have had no direct knowledge of this catastrophic event.**[2] ✋ What is the point Tillers is trying to make here? It is that, although the flow of images is always *actually* from the metropolis to the provinces, it is always possible to interpret it *virtually* as proceeding from the provinces to the metropolis. By virtue of the very fact that we receive information late and second-hand, we are empowered to read it in our own particular way, as though it were responding to our own needs and concerns. (Thus, looking at Böcklin's painting today, after the massacre of the Tasmanian Aborigines, we cannot help but interpret it as though it were painted *after* this, in the full knowledge of this 'catastrophic event'.) And the possibility of this reversibility is ineradicable: it is this always *virtual* two-way communication that allows any *actual* one-way traffic, either from the metropolis to the provinces or from the provinces to the metropolis. That is to say, Tillers is not *actually* opposing anything to the movement of information and images from the metropolis to the provinces, to the domination of the metropolis over the provinces. For him, this reality is incontestable; even to reverse the situation would only be to make the provinces the new metropolis and the metropolis the new provinces. Rather, what he is implying is an always *virtual* possibility — that of this reality's reversibility — which must accompany any actual 'transference' from one place to another, and which, in a way, makes it possible. ✋ We might find some kind of embodiment of these ideas in the image Tillers has chosen for this exhibition, *Dievturi,* painted in 1990. What we see there is the word 'faith', reproduced in a typeface adapted from the American conceptual artist Ed Ruscha, laid on top of a frieze of overlapping and intertwined hands silhouetted in charcoal. The work — whose title translates roughly as 'The Keepers of the Gods' in Tillers's native Latvian — might be understood as a reference to a remarkable series of historical events Tillers is fond of quoting. On 27 August 1989 one million Latvians, Lithuanians and Estonians, then under Soviet rule, were inspired by the Lithuanian president, Vytautas Landsbergis, to join hands and form a 680–kilometre human chain, which ran from Tallinn, the capital of Estonia, in the north-east, to Vilnius, the capital of Lithuania, in the south-west. This extraordinary gesture of protest became known as the 'Baltic Way'. By the end of 1989, the Soviet empire had begun to crumble. In June 1990 the Russian president Mikhail Gorbachev, was forced to visit Vilnius to try to prevent the Lithuanian Communist Party from leaving the Soviet Union; on 11 March 1991 Latvia declared itself a free and independent country; and on 16 August 1991 Gorbachev was himself ousted as president, and Communist rule was ended in Russia.[3] ✋ The question Tillers asks (it is the same question he poses with regard to the connection between Böcklin's painting and the massacre of the Tasmanian Aborigines) is this: can this symbolic action — not coincidentally inspired by the Lithuanian-born Fluxus artist George Maciunas, a personal friend of Landsbergis — be seen as responsible for the fall of Communism? In something analogous to the 'failure of locality' we observe in quantum mechanics, where the results of one experimenter can seem to affect the results of another experimenter in another 'space-like separated' area, or to that 'butterfly effect' in chaos theory, where a small input into a highly sensitive system can produce a catastrophic and entirely disproportionate effect, can we say that this purely symbolic action, which took place only on the level of the virtual, actually led to the liberation of millions of people from fifty years of Soviet rule? In a way, just as with Tillers's earlier speculations, we cannot deny the possibility. It is always open to us to read events in this order or as having this causal link, to imagine that it was not Russia which dominated the Baltic States for all those years but the Baltic States which in fact held the key to Russia. ✋ And is this not always the role of art: not to intervene directly in the world but to provide a totally different explanation of it; not to offer a necessarily partial account of events but, a little like that 'butterfly effect', to be that tiny crystal around which a whole world precipitates? Art should not actually enter the world but *double* it: it should not seek to become real but to give another entirely virtual explanation of the real, something which, at the same time, follows the real completely and occupies an absolutely different space from it. The world changes not as a result of action, but of thought. And Tillers's art — like all great thought — proposes a hypothesis about the world which necessarily makes itself true; which the world, in its very reality, can only verify. (To say that Böcklin's painting can only be read in terms of the massacre of the Tasmanian Aborigines is to make it so; the suggestion that the fall of Communism occurred as a result of the 'Baltic Way' henceforth is undeniable.) In a sense, the role of art is precisely to produce coincidence, to make us see what is in a new light, as though it were destined or fated in this way from the very beginning. (Böcklin's painting is *already* about the massacre of the Tasmanian Aborigines; events in Russia have *always* followed those in the Baltic States.) This is what it means to say that art gives life meaning: art at once merely repeats or follows life, but life does not exist before this repetition — just as the ordinary course of events means nothing until that coincidence which catches it up — after which, of course, it was the first event which already contained the second, that first event which already hinted at the second. ✋ This is why the virtual reality of art is always superior to the 'virtual reality' of machines. The 'virtual reality' of machines — telephones, computers, faxes — is only ever real: it only deals with the world on the level of the empirical, the actual, the linear. Whereas, as Tillers's art shows, the true reality of the world is always non-empirical, virtual, reversible. It is the undecidable and unpredictable — the unexpected relationship of one event to another, of one text to another — that is the true reality of the world. And it is this reality which could never finally be appropriated or coded by machines, no matter how powerful, because every classification would always open up the possibility of its reversibility and inversion. No matter how many connections are actually made and entered into the system of telecommunications — and there would be theoretically no limit to these — there would always be more possibilities outside of them. ✋ It is for this reason that we might say of that word 'faith' in Tillers's painting that, although it is always actually appropriated, although somebody always actually speaks in its name, it could never be completely appropriated, its potential effects could never be definitively used up; it always speaks of a certain openness to any totalitarian system, whether it be a communist dictatorship or the capitalist image-bank. We might speak in this regard of the 'good' infinity of the Mallarméan book, which is immediate and reversible, as opposed to the 'bad' infinity of the modern computer, which is merely additive and linear. It might be for this reason that machines will never really be able to think or make art: they can only interpret events in the order in which they occurred or in terms of their objective importance. They are always too accurate, too indebted to the reality of the world. Art plays another game entirely: that of proposing statements that make themselves true, which double the world and force us to see things in an absolutely new way. Art introduces novelty and difference into the world, breaks with the endless chain of empirical causality and gives the world a reality, which is, ultimately, the only one it has: that of an always virtual undemonstrable yet irrefutable 'fiction'.

rex butler

Imants Tillers *Dievturi*. 1990 charcoal, synthetic polymer paint on 48 canvasboards each 12.6 x 16.7 cm, Nos 30272–30319 76.0 x 142.0 cm. Private Collection, United States, Photo courtesy of the artist

references

1. *Imants Tillers, 'Locality Fails', Art & Text, No. 6, Winter 1982, p.55.* **2.** *Ibid., p.57.* **3.** *Imants Tillers, 'Turbulence in the Image Field', paper presented at the conference Under Capricorn, The Museum of New Zealand, Wellington, February–March 1994 (unpublished).*

ETERNITY

Calvin Klein

VIR
TUAL
REAL
ITY

NATIONAL GALLERY OF AUSTRALIA
10 DECEMBER 1994 – 5 FEBRUARY 1995

If we came across the *Freiland* photographs in a magazine like *National Geographic*, they might initially appear quite straightforward. One could read them as a photo-essay on a Turkish meeting place in Kreuzberg where the Berlin wall used to be. 'Freiland' is the term for the vacant space previously occupied by the wall: land that has been 'freed' from its role of dividing Berlin into two; land that remains 'free' until its public usage is determined. ● Kreuzberg, which was once the furthermost stretch of West Berlin, is now near Berlin's geographical heart. It is home to a large Turkish population. There, in *Freiland*, a few Turkish families have constructed their own meeting place adjacent to a large garden plot where they grow vegetables and flowers. ● But after turning a page or two, Janet Burchill and Jennifer McCamley's *Freiland* would begin to falter as photo-journalism. There are too many pictures. (The conventional photo-essay is concise; it condenses the complexities of experience into a few key images.) And these pictures are technically imperfect. Their distorted colour is a result of the artists' deliberate use of some old film stock — hence the conspicuous magenta cast. Even more disorienting is the obstinate emptiness of the pictures and the lack of human drama that has come to typify contemporary photo-journalism. ● And what of *Freiland's* relationship to documentary photography, some of whose tropes it also mimics? Certainly, Burchill and McCamley's project involved the documentation of a particular site and time. During the fourteen months they photographed the Turkish meeting place it was being constantly re-fashioned by its owners with the spoils scavenged from the newly renovated neighbouring flats in former East Berlin. In the pictures one notes the comings and goings of finds such as a large teddy bear and a carpet pinned up in triumph like a flag, as well as more 'permanent' fixtures such as chicken wire and an inscrutable pile of sand. (This is not to say that any significance can be construed either from the objects depicted or of the relations between them — they assume equal weight, but not as information.) ● The documentation of time is equally unfixed, shifting between the particular and general. Those prominent broken-down black and white flower chairs have a contemporary history: fresh from the scrapheap, apparently they were very fashionable items of furniture in the former Democratic Republic in the late 1980s. Time's more general passage is marked by the differences in light and the changing seasons that leave behind their traces on the construction. ● *Freiland* may resemble a documentary project but it does not fulfil the standard promises of documentary photography. What information do these photographs give us? What do we 'learn' from them? ● Burchill and McCamley's photographs are, in fact, mute — echoing Burchill's previously stated interest (in 1988) 'in a quality of opacity, in the obtuseness of images, a muting of their communicative potential'.[1] Within this context *Freiland* may make more 'sense'. ● Two close-ups of patterned furniture fabric: freed from any representational or narrative imperatives, are like blank screens across which flicker a myriad of references to other photographs. William Henry Fox Talbot's beautiful, almost fugitive image of lace (taken in the 1840s) may come to mind; or a whole flood of ethnographic photographs whose specific function is descriptive — of material, of process, of culture. ● When Janet Burchill and Jennifer McCamley first arrived in Berlin in 1992 for a one-year residency at the Künstlerhaus Bethanien, they were considering 'making work which dealt with architectural spaces of different historical periods and styles'.[2] The Turkish families' construction offered them an unexpected way of dealing with these concerns, but one that has a certain logic in the light of their previous art practice.[3] ● Though built pragmatically to meet personal and social needs, the Turkish meeting place was appreciated by Burchill and McCamley as a work of art: **[We] were struck by both the art tropes so evident in it (from Bauhaus to a down market John Armlender) and its beauty as a sculpture/assemblage.**[4] ● The construction was unwittingly a pastiche in which numerous modernist art references could be discerned[5] — even in the very means used to cobble together the different elements. The artists observed that the cement bases moulded for some pieces of furniture 'acted almost like plinths to display these objects so awry from their original "form and function"'.[6] ● Indeed, the artists' comment may come as no suprise: that 'people often presume that we made this ourselves as an installation and then photographed it, as so many visual elements are so close to art concerns'.[7] ● The invitation to the viewer in *Freiland* is open-ended: 'the motifs in the photographs are detailed sufficiently to be open to a large number of perceptions and interpretations'.[8] There are no definitive pictures, none stands singly as a summation for the whole. Nor is there any pretence of a master narrative. ● As I look at the *Freiland* photographs — which, it should be said, are not magazine reproductions at all but large-scale prints with an impressive physical presence[9] — I am taken by an unremarkable detail: a cigarette butt lying stubbed out on the ground. Recently smoked, not yet rotted down, it conjures up an image of a body that never materialises.

The occupants of 'Freiland' are invisible — ripe for displacement when the capitalist economy claims the free land on which they temporarily squat.

helen ennis

references

1. *Janet Burchill in an interview with Peter Cripps*, Stephen Bush. Janet Burchill. *The Lewers Bequest and Penrith Regional Art Gallery, Sydney, 1988, exhibition catalogue, p.16.* **2.** *Jennifer McCamley and Janet Burchill in a letter to Mary Eagle, 2 July 1994, p.1, National Gallery of Australia, Registry file 92/33.* **3.** *I am thinking here particularly of Burchill's use of what she has described as 'modernist emblems such as the cross; roses (via Gertrude Stein), white on white; red, yellow and blue'. See interview with Peter Cripps, p.16.* **4.** *Letter to Mary Eagle, p.2.* **5.** *For example, in the furniture (the chrome frames of the dining chairs mimic the revolutionary stainless steel furniture produced at the Bauhaus in the 1920s), and in the arrangments of objects whose abstract shapes and colours recall the paintings of Piet Mondrian.* **6.** *Letter to Mary Eagle, p.2.* **7.** *Ibid., p.3.* **8.** *Ibid., p.3.* **9.** *McCamley and Burchill write of the 'defamiliarisation' they aim for in the museum installation of* Freiland: *'The two different sizes of the photographs, the interspersal of a few vertical shots and the hanging on one line rather than the standard option of centring the photographs bring about a slight defamiliarisation which does not turn the work into the easy option of a photographic installation but embodies an architectonics transmuted into a demographics.' Letter to Mary Eagle, p.3.*

JANET BURCHILL & JENNIFER MCCAMLEY

janet burchill and **jennifer mccamley**, *Freiland.* (detail) 1992–93 19 type-C photographs. National Gallery of Australia. Purchased 1994

RONALD JONES

CONTAGION CULTURES

Through painstaking research and meticulous fabrication Ronald Jones re-configures sculpture for the Information Age. His sculptures are made to tell stories that pointedly undermine our expectations; narratives of barbarism, cruelty or fear are revealed beneath the implacable surfaces of the mute objects of the modern world — chairs, tables, trestles, military maps and artificial hearts. In so doing, Jones points to the extreme limitation of Modernism's privileging of perceptual cues over contextual clues; the information provided in his sculptures' extended titles denies any simple relationship between style and content.

This has never been clearer than in a group of five sculptures produced by Jones in 1988–89 which appear to be examples of Modernist abstraction as exemplified by the work of Constantin Brancusi and Jean Arp. Yet these works are also based on biological and microscopic imagery of the HIV virus and the genetic structure of cancer. Working with scientists and doctors in the field and using data gathered through high-tech imaging techniques, Jones looked at sculptures by Brancusi and Arp alongside images of the HIV virus and the DNA structure of cancer cells. Finding strong morphological similarities between the sculptures and the scientific data, Jones matched them up. Submitting the 2-D scientific imagery to computer manipulation, he came up with virtual 3-D models of sculptures which were then fabricated to correspond to the exemplar sculpture. *Untitled (DNA fragment from human chromosome 13 carrying mutant Rb genes also known as malignant oncogenes which trigger rapid cancer tumorigenesis)* 1989 in the permanent collection of the National Gallery of Australia is in fact based on Jean Arp's *Leaf torso* of 1963. The resulting sculpture remains true to Arp's; however, morphologically it is based on the cancerous DNA.[1] Where Arp's sculpture is loosely based on the

sinuous curves of the human torso whose tripartite structure dynamically thrusts upward, Jones's sculpture seems to be dividing across the middle, its dynamism expended in self-replication. By producing a 'virtual' Arp, Jones has confounded the values of the Modernist sculpture on which his work is based.

In fact, one could say that the values of Arp and Brancusi's abstractions have been clinically inverted by Jones who has written along these same lines:

My sculptures take hostage Arp and Brancusi's intuitive search for a higher modern form, a utopic or perfect order and pervert it into something distressed or dying, a promise unkept to the culture at large ... These sculptures foreground the way disease has become a political subject, a subject that reminds us all of what it means to be dispossessed in our culture. That these sculptures appear as the stylistic antithesis to the earlier geometric work is important. This is an intentional rupture in style designed to confound and interrupt one of art history's most important narratives: the trail of stylistic development and the sacredness of evolutionary aesthetics.[2]

Where Modernist abstractions of the human form often represent an intuitive quest for eternal symbolic form, Jones's viruses have everything to do with the limits of mortality. Where Arp and Brancusi embraced dynamism in a utopian generative sense, Jones's viral dynamism is inwardly directed and destructive. Jones's sculptures present an image of a Modernism that ceaselessly self-replicates, feeding upon itself, pursuing tighter and tighter limits until despite its dynamic rhetoric it has all but ceased to be a force for social change.

It is not insignificant, however, that his sculptures appear to be virtually equivalent to the objects that he is interrogating. Jones's sculptures operate like a cancer in that they present themselves to the body of Modernism as something

ronald jones

Untitled (DNA fragment from human chromosome 13 carrying mutant Rb genes also known as malignant oncogenes which trigger rapid cancer tumorigenesis). 1989 bronze 200.0 x 22.8 x 22.8 cm. National Gallery of Australia. Purchased 1993

that they are not. It is only after these sculptures have insinuated themselves into the gallery through this masquerade of Modernist detachment and self-sufficiency that discontinuities emerge. These are finally revealed with precision and cool in his essayistic titles which, despite their disturbing content, are delivered entirely without adjectives, without judgement. This is true even where the information contained in the title is more socially confrontational than in the viral sculptures, as in *Untitled (Edward Earl Johnson sat in this side chair as he ate his last meal before being executed in the lethal gas chamber at the Mississippi State penitentiary at 12:06 am on May 20, 1987. His meal included shrimp cocktail, something Johnson had not eaten before. The music box played 'Always' by Atlantic Star. Johnson's family sang 'Always' to him during their final visit a few hours before his execution. The lyrics of this song include the passage: 'You're the perfect one, for me it forever will be, and I love you so for always'.)* 1990. The objects ingratiate themselves to the gallery through their look or style, while his extended titles always point the way outside.

Even so, because of the precision of Jones's language his work never lapses into didacticism; instead, we are presented with a politically charged aesthetics for the information age. In the feedback loop produced by exposing Modernism to the flows of information that it often suppresses, its calm surfaces — from its utopian sculpture to the anonymity of its architecture and furniture — glow with an almost psychotic intensity. Careful, it might just be contagious.

trevor smith

references

1. *I am indebted to the artist for generously providing the information about his source material and working methods. Information contained in correspondence from the artist, 14 July 1994.*
2. *Ibid.*

EDWARD RUSCHA

Ruscha's paintings are about words. He hasn't attempted to figure out the meanings of words, although his work does impart the slipperiness of such an endeavour. Ruscha's paintings have given words size ('You can make them any size, and what's the real size? Nobody knows'[1]) and noise (loud and soft); have made them wet, sharp, gooey, sticky, prickly, violent, friendly, unsettling, cold or hot. **D** *Words have temperatures to me. When they reach a certain point and become hot words, then they appeal to me. 'Synthetic' is a very hot word. Sometimes I have a dream that if a word gets too hot and too appealing, it will boil apart, and I won't be able to read or think of it. Usually I catch them before they get too hot.*[2] **D** Words, as we know from life, have a life in reality — the world of our physical experience. They exist as actual markers, as signs on billboards, buses, buildings. Ruscha's photobook, *Twentysix Gasoline Stations* 1962, makes this clear: STANDARD, spelled out atop a gas station, proclaims itself as a word and as a marker. Similarly, FOUNTAIN BLU, in cursive script across the front of an apartment block (photographed by Ruscha for his *Some Los Angeles Apartments* 1965), acts in the same way. It has been suggested on several occasions that Ruscha's paintings are intimately linked with the place of their execution — Los Angeles,[3] but the work itself betrays this straightforward interpretation. Despite the objects that they are attached to, the words exist independently. This is signalled by Ruscha in paintings like *Blue collar tires* 1992, depicting a blocky concrete building with the word TIRES in capital letters along one side. While the gas stations, apartments and auto shops really exist, Ruscha points out the independent life of the words that adorn them. Another painting of a similar blocky building, is lettered with TOOL & DIE. The fact that this is not a real building is beside the point, as Ruscha states: 'Just the phrase "tool & die" is enough to handle itself.'[4]

D For Ruscha, the simple act of painting words emphasises their status as objects. Like the STANDARD gas station sign, Ruscha's paintings exist in real space. Ruscha's words, however, move beyond the materiality of their medium: they are both metaphorical and objectified. **D** From his earliest work, Ruscha has exposed the psychological characteristics of words. *Sweetwater,* painted in 1959, spells out its name across the canvas in neat capital letters with serifs. It is, in a sense, existentialist. Although we simultaneously read Ruscha's words, and look at them, the two activities taken together are often unhelpful. For example, we all know the meaning of the word MURDER, but what does it mean to see it painted with spinach juice; or how do we interpret words painted in egg yolk, carrot juice, gunpowder or tobacco? Even when Ruscha uses regular types of paint, there are no more clues: RANCHO is painted with a verisimilitude that is maple syrup; MOTOR is drawn so that the letters look like strips of white paper. **D** The diversity of media Ruscha was using in the 1970s acted to open up a broad field of semantic multivalency. The strategy of alerting the viewer (or reader) to their reliance on the structuring devices of language is first signalled in these works. Ruscha makes it increasingly difficult to pin down any kind of final and definitive meaning in his words. It has been suggested that he actually liquidates meaning, that he is 'interested in the inherent uncertainty of

signification — its great potential for failure'.[5] Rather than enforcing nihilism, however, I would suggest that Ruscha recognises and capitalises on the abstract nature of words; he exposes the ambiguity of a trait that is fundamental to our recognition and perception of most objects, and our reliance and expectation of underlying structures that shape our understanding of significance and meaning. **D** Ruscha has sometimes set his words against the reality from which they are drawn. *Canada, U.S.A, Mexico* 1980 places the words above a gently curving horizon, in *Talk radio* 1987 they float in the sky above a grid of city lights. In *Chain and cable* 1987 they are suspended in front of a fuzzy monochrome image of a sailing ship tossed on the ocean.[6] More often than not, Ruscha's words simply float in space, a space that is: *absolute surface and absolute depth, to which words react, through which for a spell they turn away from their meaning to operate in a dimension both concrete and abstract. The theorem might run as follows: a thing is concrete only insofar as it is abstract. In reality, meaning and image cut across each other on numerous levels: the ambivalence is constant.*[7] **D** Ruscha makes evident the extent to which we rely on the structures that regulate visual and written language, and how it is via the expectation of the existence of these structures that the viewer/reader searches for a logic and a meaning. Ruscha's work, by necessitating and then thwarting this expectation, alerts us to its existence and offers us the possibility of countering it. He inaugurates an open-ended indefiniteness of the text. Ruscha fractures and slices open the link between signifier and signified, opening up a space where interpretation and meaning reside only in ourselves. **D** We each may have our own destiny, but Ruscha's painting of the word DESTINY releases us from any obligations. While Sylvie Fleury's deployment of the word ETERNITY flips the word over twice (from semantics to consumerism and back again), it is always anchored to the system that is the object of her critique. Similarly, Imants Tillers use of the word FAITH traffics in irony: it is Tillers's imagery that reveals the double edge of pathos and hope. Ruscha's DESTINY, instead, is an unfixed one. A word that is at once innocent and frightening becomes unhinged from its meaning. This is not to say that it is silenced; on the contrary, it is made all the more rich through Ruscha's stripping it of attendant interpretive devices. **D** Ruscha exercises the right of remaking reality, and his art alerts the viewer to this same possibility.

christopher chapman

references

1. Edward Ruscha in Fred Fehlau, 'Ed Ruscha', Flash Art, No. 138, January/February 1988, p.70. **2.** Edward Ruscha in Howardena Pindell, 'Words with Ruscha', The Print Collector's Newsletter, Vol. 3, No. 6, January/February 1973, p.126. Quoted by Yve-Alain Bois, 'Thermometers Should Last Forever', Edward Ruscha: Romance With Liquids, Paintings 1966–1969, New York: Rizzoli/Gagosian Gallery, 1993, p.20. **3.** See for instance Dave Hickey's 'Available Light', in The Works of Edward Ruscha, New York: Hudson Hills Press/San Francisco Museum of Modern Art, 1982, pp. 18–31; Judi Freeman's 'Edward Ruscha' in LA Pop in the Sixties, Newport Harbour Art Museum, Newport Beach, 1989, exhibition catalogue, pp. 124–133; and Richard Marshall's Edward Ruscha: Los Angeles Apartments, Whitney Museum of American Art, New York, 1990. **4.** Edward Ruscha, 'A Conversation between Walter Hopps and Edward Ruscha', in Edward Ruscha: Romance with Liquids, Paintings 1966–1969, p.108. **5.** Donald Kuspit, 'Signs in Suspense', Arts Magazine, Vol. 54, No. 8, April 1991, p.54. **6.** Ruscha's more recent paintings sometimes dispense with words altogether. His use of a floating 'space-bar' in front of silhouetted images continues to refer to words, but through their absence. A group of paintings from 1991 appear like stills from black-and-white movies, the images as paradoxically open-ended as Ruscha's use of words. **7.** Alain Cueff, 'Edward Ruscha: A Distant World', Parkett, No. 18, 1988, p.59.

edward ruscha from *Twentysix Gasoline Stations.* 1962 artist's book, offset lithography 17.8 x 14.0 cm. National Gallery of Australia. Purchased 1981
edward ruscha *Destiny.* 1990 oil on canvas 60.0 x 80.0 cm Collection Stephen Hurowitz, New York. Courtesy Thomas Segal Gallery, Boston, and Barbara Krakow Gallery, Boston

VIR
TUAL
REAL
ITY

NATIONAL GALLERY OF AUSTRALIA
· 10 DECEMBER 1994 – 5 FEBRUARY 1995